FATHER ALLAN

Roger Hutchinson is an award-winning author and journalist. After working as an editor in London, in 1977 he joined the *West Highland Free Press* in Skye. Since then he has published fifteen books, including *Polly: the True Story Behind Whisky Galore*. He is still attached to the *WHFP* as a columnist, and has written for BBC Radio, *The Scotsman*, *The Guardian*, *The Herald* and *The Literary Review*. His book *The Soap Man* (Birlinn 2003) was shortlisted for the Saltire Scottish Book of the Year (2004) and his best-selling *Calum's Road* was shortlisted for the Ondaatje Prize (2007).

FATHER ALLAN

The Life and Legacy of a Hebridean Priest

Roger Hutchinson

BIRLINN

First published in 2010 by
Birlinn Limited
West Newington House
10 Newington Road
Edinburgh
EH9 1QS

www.birlinn.co.uk

ISBN: 978 1 84158 548 2

British Library Cataloguing-in-Publication Data
A catalogue record for this book is available from the British Library

Typeset by Edderston Book Design, Peebles
Printed and bound by CPI Cox & Wyman Ltd, Reading

CONTENTS

LIST OF ILLUSTRATIONS

Father Allan MacDonald of Eriskay

Blairs Seminary on Deeside

A group of pupils at Blairs in 1863, eight years before Allan MacDonald arrived there

Allan with some fellow students in Valladolid in about 1878, when he was 19 years old

The Lord of the Isles: Father Allan at sea in oilskins, crossing between South Uist and Eriskay

Sagart Mor nan Each, Father John Mackintosh of Bornish

Father George Rigg of Daliburgh

The old St Michael's Church in Eriskay, with Father Allan sitting on a rock before it

The new St Michael's Church in Eriskay

Island and mainland clergymen from the Diocese of Argyll and the Isles at the consecration of the new St Michael's Church in May 1903

'It was on Sunday mornings that the whole island turned out'

A group of Eriskay women waulking tweed and singing their worksongs, as their priest looks on

Father Allan MacDonald as his congregation knew him, at the age of 39 in 1898

PREFACE

In July 2009 the South Uist arts organisation Ceolas held in the island of Eriskay a four-day Gaisgeach an t-Sluaigh (Champion of the People) symposium on the life and work of Father Allan MacDonald. The sun shone on a perfect event. The symposium was opened by Eriskay's Freeman of the Western Isles – and self-confessed 'oldest Eriskay man still living in Eriskay' – Father Calum MacLellan.

The broadcasters Angela MacKinnon, herself of Eriskay, and Jo MacDonald of Lewis discussed, with the help of some local ladies, the life of Eriskay during Father Allan's time, and his unique collection of Gaelic words and phrases from South Uist and Eriskay. Dr Roddy Campbell of Lochboisdale delivered a witty address on typhus and other viruses which struck down islanders 100 years ago, and Father Michael MacDonald of Bornish explored – with the help of Father Allan's diaries – the intriguing detail of his priestly life and colleagues in the Southern Isles.

Magda Sagarzazu and Hugh Cheape plundered the Canna archives left by John Lorne Campbell to offer photographic and literary insights into the great priest's friends and visitors. The proceeds culminated with a scholarly and entertaining workshop by Isabel T. MacDonald, with the assistance of Paul MacCallum and other singers, on Father Allan's enduring Gaelic hymns.

I owe a debt to Ceolas and to all of the people mentioned above. That symposium crystallised what had previously been my own inchoate interest in the priest from Fort William who became celebrated throughout Scotland and beyond, and whose name also became synonymous with the southern Outer Hebrides. The seminars and discussions in Eriskay School in July

2009 were dignified by the presence of several local people. A man observed at one point that during the nineteenth century the name 'Allan' was almost unknown among Eriskay boys. After 1905, however, it became commonplace. Much of this book is an attempt to discover why.

The late John Lorne Campbell of Canna had a fascination with Allan MacDonald that stopped short of preparing a long written life. John Campbell did almost everything but write a complete biography of Father Allan. He eulogised him in a short booklet. He edited and introduced the diaries of Frederick Rea, in which Father Allan featured strongly. He examined in *Strange Things* the bizarre relationships between the Society for Psychical Research, Ada Goodrich-Freer and Father Allan MacDonald. He collated and prefaced the priest's collection of Gaelic words and expressions for publication. He amassed memorabilia. He pursued Allan MacDonald's own explorations of Hebridean folklore.

But John Campbell did not write the book. Somehow that task fell to me. Any merit in this product can be attributed in part to the author's nervous awareness of the shade of the scholar of Canna House gazing critically over his shoulder.

Ronald Black, another specialist in the work of Allan Mac-Donald and the editor of his collected poems and hymns, who is presently preparing Father Allan's residual folklore collection for publication, was characteristically helpful and supportive. The Gaelic–English translations of Allan MacDonald's verse and songs are all taken from Ronnie's anthology *Eilein na h-Oige*. I am deeply grateful for Ronnie Black's forensic reading of my manuscript, and his correction of many important details and insertion of others.

Andrew Nicoll of the Scottish Catholic Archives in Edinburgh directed me into useful, dusty corners. My old friend Cailean Maclean patiently corrected my geography and my Gaelic. The survey of nineteenth-century Gaelic usage throughout Scotland conducted and collated by Kurt C. Duwe was invaluable. Davie McClymont and Morna MacLaren of Portree Public Library located and obtained for me rare books and pamphlets. Thanks also to Hugh Andrew and Andrew Simmons of Birlinn, that brilliant book jacket designer Jim Hutcheson, my editor Helen Bleck and my agent, Stan, of Jenny Brown Associates.

Most of all I must thank the two contemporary Hebridean Roman Catholic priests who illuminated the 2009 Ceolas symposium. Father Michael J. MacDonald of Bornish has been generous to a fault with his time, his judgement and his own researches. Father Calum MacLellan of Eriskay was always a wise and witty host at the priest's house once occupied by Allan MacDonald and a perfect guide to the church which he built, to the island that both men have loved, and to the best qualities of Highland clergymen. None of the people mentioned above are responsible for any inadequacies, errors or misrepresentations in this biography.

Like most other people with the surname MacDonald, Father Allan spelt it himself and saw it written in at least four different ways. In this book I have retained the different versions used by others in their quoted stories of him and other members of Clan Donald, but in my own narrative I have dispensed with McDonald, Mcdonald and Macdonald and used MacDonald throughout, for no reasons other than consistency.

Roger Hutchinson
May 2010

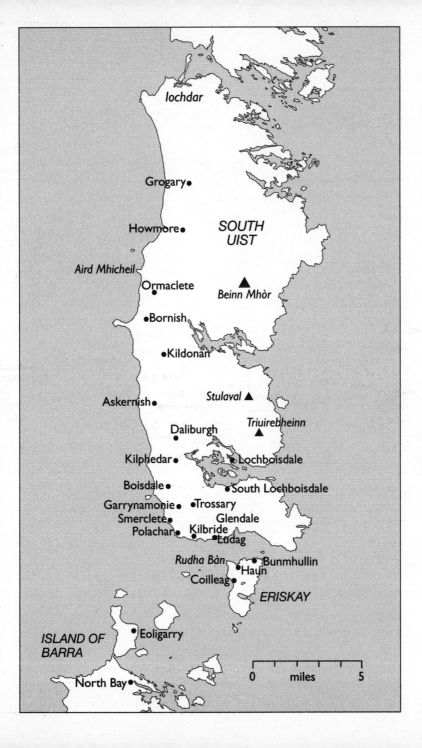

OCTOBER 1905

Glasgow Herald, 14 October 1905

Amid ceremonial that was touched with pathos and yet was not without more than a little of the romantic and picturesque, the mortal remains of Father Allan MacDonald, the famous priest and scholar of Eriskay, were on Thursday laid in the grave.

The lonely island so far from the heart and hum of human things was a scene of weeping. The entire population is of the Roman Catholic faith, the ancient religion of Eriskay never having been interrupted by the Reformation upheaval, and for its spiritual and no less its material wellbeing Father Allan had lived and toiled.

He was not only the priest but the staff upon whom everyone leant, the kindly advisor to whom everyone turned; and the hand of death in removing him has laid a heavy blow upon the little remote community that he loved so well and that loved him in return.

Born in Lochaber, he desired that he should lie in the island where he had laboured so long and so zealously, and within hearing of the swell of the Atlantic. He pointed out the spot three years ago and recalled it with perfect clarity shortly before he died.

The funeral was an unforgettable sight. No fewer than twenty-one priests crossed the seas of the Minch to be there, the whole of the islanders were mourners and Father Allan went to his long rest amid the tears of strong men not used to weeping.

Not only Eriskay, but a wide world of friends lament the death of this heroic, humble-spirited priest and greatest of Celtic scholars and lorists.

1

THE POST-HORN

*≈ 'Many a person was regaled by him with old lore
and tales that lightened their journey for them.' ≈*

A few years before Allan MacDonald was born in 1859, his father
worked as a coach guard.

John MacDonald was responsible for safety and comfort on
the Marquess of Breadalbane stagecoach in the Scottish Highlands; he would perch, wearing livery of scarlet and gold, with a
blunderbuss and pistols in the outside rear box of the coach. The
blunderbuss would be, according to a Highland writer in the
1850s, 'full charged to the muzzle, – not wishing harm to any one,
but bound in duty to let drive at all and sundry who would make
war upon the passengers, or attempt running the conveyance off
the road . . .'

The Marquess of Breadalbane, known colloquially as 'the
Breadalbane', was a celebrated Highland coach in the middle of
the nineteenth century. Its most usual routes were to and from
Inverarnan at the head of Loch Lomond, where it would pick
up steamer passengers who had sailed 25 miles up the loch from
the jetty at Balloch, to destinations in Perthshire and Inverness-
shire such as Aberfeldy and Fort William. The Breadalbane coach
was advertised in July 1843 as 'departing from the Head of Loch

Lomond for Fort William every Tuesday, Thursday and Saturday on the arrival of the Loch Lomond Steamer'.

From the head of Loch Lomond the coach track mainly followed the old convex, six yards-wide gravel roads which had been laid over a century earlier, between 1725 and 1737 under the direction of General George Wade, to allow the British Army to march more easily about a previously intractable region.

When John MacDonald was on the Fort William run, after boarding at Inverarnan his stage went down Glen Falloch to Crianlarich, then north through Tyndrum and Bridge of Orchy. From Bridge of Orchy it would fork left around Loch Tulla through the small community at Black Mount, across the forbidding Monadh Dubh and then spin over the wilderness of Rannoch Moor into Glencoe. It would wind down the precipitous track to Glencoe and Ballachulish villages. Passengers would dismount at the inn on the shore of the Ballachulish narrows, where Argyll was just one furlong of salt water from Lochaber. The coach, its horses, its human contents and its cargo would then be loaded separately onto the antique ferry and towed across the kyle of Loch Leven to be reunited at the other side. It finally rolled round the coast and up the southern shore of Loch Linnhe to its destination at Fort William.

It was an arduous journey. The Highland Roads and Bridges Commission reported in 1845 that:

The distance from Glasgow to Fort William has latterly been usually accomplished by travellers using the route of Loch Lomond, in about twelve or thirteen hours, reaching the head of Loch Lomond by the steam boats, and thence proceeding by the Black Mount. The commissioners have already done much upon this line, which, like the other military roads, was originally of very imperfect construction; but a very considerable outlay will still be absolutely necessary to remove the steepest of the ascents and the most sudden of the turns which abound upon it, before it can be considered safe for the rapid transit of heavily-laden stage carriages.

John MacDonald was employed directly by the Post Office to protect its mails from highway robbery. He was individually accountable for the safe delivery of the post. If the Marquess of Breadalbane lost a wheel or was stalled in any other way, John MacDonald was expected to continue to its destination with the mail, on foot or by other means. He was not allowed to leave his cargo. If there was mail on board when the Marquess of Breadalbane stopped at Crianlarich or Ballachulish, John MacDonald could not accompany the driver and passengers indoors for warmth and refreshment. Whatever the season, he had to remain with his weapons in his open-air box beside his parcels and bags. Very occasionally British stagecoach guards died from hypothermia in the execution of their duties. As a result of their heavy responsibilities, and to forestall corruption, coach guards were well paid and handsomely pensioned.

Coach guards were naturally familiar with their territory and the people on their routes were familiar with them. In a twentieth-century obituary of his son Allan, it was recalled that John MacDonald had been 'for many years the highly-respected conductor of the once famous four-in-hand coach which ran between Fort William, via Glencoe and Blackmount, to Glasgow. He and Duncan MacMaster, the famous driver, were two well-known personalities on this route.' In 1933 a Skyeman of a later generation imputed to John MacDonald some of the interests for which his son Allan would become celebrated, writing that the Breadalbane conductor 'was closely acquainted with everyone whom he would meet on the long and difficult road that used to wend its way through those bounds at that time, and many a person was regaled by him with old lore and tales that lightened their journey for them.'

John MacDonald's blunderbuss and other weapons were largely

ceremonial. Pedestrians were occasionally ambushed, but there were no highway robberies of coaches in the Highlands in the middle of the nineteenth century. Passengers and cargo on the routes north of Loch Lomond at that time were safer from molestation than those on the Dover Road out of London or the Glasgow to Edinburgh turnpike.

Most people in Fort William would have heard John Mac-Donald arrive before they saw him. The most vivid residual public memory of coach guards was only realised when the stagecoaches had gone and been replaced in all quarters of the British Isles by the faster, warmer, drier and safer railway trains.

As well as his armoury, each coach guard was equipped with a post-horn. He blew a peremptory series of blasts, usually before entering a township, to warn toll-keepers to open their gates, posthouses to open their doors, and other traffic and pedestrians to get out of the way of Her Majesty's Mail. From Fort William in the north-west to Folkestone in the south-east, that sound was for two centuries as familiar a feature of muted British rural life as the chiming of church bells. It was the 'rapid crescendo of the coach guard's horn' which 'wakens the echoes of the place', whose sudden absence was lamented in 1890 by the Scottish essayist George Eyre-Todd.

John MacDonald was well qualified to be a coach guard. He came from a family of carters. When he worked as the guard on the stagecoach Marquess of Breadalbane in the early 1850s, John was in his late 20s and early 30s. He was a bachelor and still living with his parents in Fort William. But his parents had only moved back to the Lochaber district in their later years.

John's father, Allan MacDonald, was known as Ailean Og (Young Allan), which in turn gave John himself the patronymic of Iain Ailein Oig (John of Young Allan). Allan MacDonald was born in 1782 in the huge rural parish of Kilmonivaig, which stretched from Appin in the south to Glenshiel and Glenmoriston in the north, from Laggan in the east to Glenelg in the west, and which included the two central townships of Spean Bridge and Invergarry. The parish of Kilmonivaig spread across four different counties (Inverness-shire, Argyllshire, Ross-shire and Perthshire) and in the nineteenth century was larger than most of the Lowland Scottish shires. Allan was born in the Inverness-shire section of Kilmonivaig, which suggests the Lochaber region to the north of Fort William. Allan MacDonald was one of the MacDonalds of Keppoch, an old Lochaber clan which fell on hard times after the defeat of the 1745 Jacobite Rising at the Battle of Culloden just 36 years before Allan MacDonald was born. The original seat of the MacDonalds of Keppoch was at Torr Lunndaidh, two miles north of the British Army garrison called Fort William.

But Allan MacDonald did not stay at home for long. Early in the nineteenth century he became a roving carter. He met, presumably while travelling, a woman called Elizabeth MacPherson from Cromdale, 60 miles away on the eastern fringes of Inverness-shire, where the Highland hills begin to descend to the English- and Doric-speaking plains of Moray, Banff and Buchan. They married, Elizabeth MacDonald joined her husband in the haulage business and they set up house in her local parish of Inverallan, possibly a short walk from Cromdale in the planned new town of Grantown-on-Spey, which had been founded 50 years earlier.

Their sons and daughters were born there, on the north-eastern fringe of the shrinking Scottish Gaidhealtachd. John MacDonald arrived in 1821 and, like his younger brothers Ranald and Allan, as soon as he was able he joined the family business.

A carter's job was to move heavy goods by horse and cart. There were town carters in the urban conurbations, whose delivery work rarely took them outside the city streets and who survived well into the twentieth century. There were farm carters, who were usually hired hands directed to drive agricultural produce about their employer's estate. Given their location and their apparent independence, it is probable that the MacDonalds were freelance distance carters who owned their own carthorses and packhorses and equipment and were contracted to export materials from one part of Scotland to another. They often also carried passengers for extremely cheap fares – cheap because those passengers had to squat beside cargo on the cart's open flat-bed, and because there was no tax payable on personnel who were transported at less than four miles per hour. There was little more to it than that. They were the wheels of commerce. But as they operated in the north and north-west of Scotland the MacDonalds had to negotiate some of the most difficult tracks through some of the most hostile terrain in the wettest and windiest climate in northern Europe. The MacDonald family would have been strong, tough people in an age of hard outdoorsmen and women.

They ran their haulage operation out of the parish of Inverallan until the later 1830s, by which time Allan MacDonald was in his fifties and Elizabeth in her forties, and they had three strong sons to help them carry on the business. As it was by nature an itinerant business they were able then to return as a family to the Lochaber of Allan's birth. They bought a house by the shore on Low Street in Fort William. Ranald and young Allan in their late teens and twenties continued as carters, their older brother John got that prized job as guard on the Marquess of Breadalbane stagecoach, their younger sister Mary found work as a domestic servant, and their parents Allan and Elizabeth were able to retire looking over the sheltered waters of Loch Linnhe and the distant Sunart hills.

While John was working on the Breadalbane in the early 1850s, a young woman named Margaret MacPherson and her elderly mother Charlotte were staying with their relatives Alexander and Mary MacIntosh in a village at the foot of the immense shoulder of Ben Nevis just north of Fort William called Torlundy – the same Torr Lunndaidh which had been the seat of the MacDonalds of Keppoch. The MacPhersons were originally from Laggan, 20 miles to the north-east on Upper Speyside. Their deceased husband and father had been a Badenoch shepherd and farm manager named Donald MacPherson. If he was an estate employee it is unlikely that he left so much as a roof over their heads to his wife and daughter. In 1851 the widowed Charlotte was 64 years old, and her 21-year-old fatherless daughter Margaret made some money as a seamstress.

We do not know whether 30-year-old John MacDonald met 21-year-old Margaret MacPherson while he was on some carting expedition, or riding shotgun on a stage, or simply and most probably when she strolled down to Fort William from Torlundy. However they met, on 21 November 1852 they were married in Fort William, within the old parish of Kilmallie.

John then gave up both the carting business – which he left in the hands of his brothers – and the stagecoach guardsman's job. He had been able to save some money and he became a tavern-keeper on Fort William's High Street, the main thoroughfare which ran south from the town's military garrison along the first stages of the road to Rannoch Moor, Crianlarich, Loch Lomondside and Glasgow.

In 1855 Margaret gave birth to their first surviving child; a daughter whom they christened Charlotte after Margaret's mother. In 1857 a son arrived, who was called Donald, possibly after Margaret's father.

On 25 October 1859 Charlotte and Donald were given a baby brother. Nine months earlier, in January 1859, John's father Allan MacDonald, Ailean Og, had died in Fort William at the age of 77. There was only one providential name for the newborn boy. He was called Allan after his paternal grandfather.

Allan MacDonald was born in a room at his father's tavern at 179 High Street at the south-west end of Fort William. The building was torn down later in the nineteenth century and replaced by taller Victorian buildings. From the few early nineteenth-century structures which still stand in Fort William it is possible to imagine the town as it was in the 1850s and 1860s: three modest files of long, low-slung one-and-a-half-storey premises enclosing two parallel streets, each broken occasionally by a hefty three-storey granite omen of the future. The low stone walls of rectangular crofts still stretched back up the hillside behind the High Street.

Allan MacDonald grew up on the upper street, the High Street, with his back to the hill, along with his older siblings Charlotte and Donald and his younger brother and sister Ronald and Elizabeth, who were born in 1861 and 1864.

They would not have noticed at the time, when it was the only world they knew, but Fort William was a hybrid town. It was not a natural Highland development. A garrison had been established at the northern head of Loch Linnhe, by an old castle at Inverlochy, in the 1650s by forces of Oliver Cromwell's army of the Commonwealth. It was at first nothing more than a timber palisade, but it contained nine or ten companies of foot soldiers posted to a notoriously bleak and hostile part of the western Highlands.

After the Restoration and then the Glorious Revolution of 1688–89, which usurped James VII of Scotland and James II of England, the last Stuart king of Great Britain, and replaced him with the dependably Protestant William and Mary, it was deemed prudent to strengthen the garrison at Inverlochy, which stood in the middle of a number of sinewy and irredeemably Jacobite Highland clans. So barracks for 1,000 soldiers were built inside 20-foot high stone walls. In case their allegiance was mistaken by the locals, in 1690 the bastion was christened Fort William and the adjacent village was called Maryburgh. For almost two centuries neither name was accepted by most Highland Gaels. They called the fort 'Gearasdan dubh Inbhir-Lochaidh' ('The black garrison at Inverlochy'), and they let the name Maryburgh, or Baile Mairi, slip slowly out of use.

Fort William was dependent on the sea for its survival. Without the Royal Navy to provision, reinforce and defend it from the waters of Loch Linnhe, those thousand troopers could have been overwhelmed from the surrounding hills on at least two occasions during the violent eighteenth century. But by then the Highland clans had lost control of their seas, and by the end of the eighteenth century they would also have lost control of their land.

By the beginning of the nineteenth century the Highlands were effectively 'pacified'. The Jacobite rebellions had been crushed, the clan system was dissolving, emigrations both voluntary and forced were reducing the population of the Scottish Gaidhealtachd. The comfortable classes could congratulate themselves that 'There is not an instance of any country having made so sudden a change in its morals as that of the Highlands; security and civilization now possess every part; yet 30 years have not elapsed since the whole was a den of thieves of the most extraordinary kind.' An Gearasdan Dubh Inbhir-Lochaidh no longer had an active military function, and its complement was wound down. It was used as a recruiting station and as a sanitorium. As late as 1855, just four years before the birth of Allan MacDonald, it was briefly occupied by a detachment of a sergeant and 24 men of 80th Foot (Staffordshire Volunteers), who were presumably on manoeuvres. But in 1864, when Allan MacDonald was five years old, the War Office sold the fort to a local dignitary, and in 1889 most of it was demolished to make way for the new West Highland railway line and a goods yard. In 1888 the romantic novelist William Black would write:

> Peace reigns in Fort William now. Lochiel has no trouble with his clansmen; the Government have no trouble with Lochiel; the garrison buildings have been turned into private dwellings; women sit on the grassy bastions of the fort and knit stockings, sheltering themselves from the sun with an old umbrella; in the square are wooden benches for looking on at the tossing of the caber, putting the stone, and other Highland games; in the fosse is grown an excellent crop of potatoes and cabbages; and

just outside there is a trimly kept bowling-green, in which the club-members practise the gentle art of reaching the tee when the waning afternoon releases them from their desk or counter.

Indeed it is possible that [a traveller], who had visited Edinburgh once or twice, and had passed the lofty crags and castle walls of Stirling, may have been disappointed to find a place of fair historic fame with so little to show for itself; but if Fort William is not in itself picturesque, it is in the very midst of wonderfully picturesque surroundings.

The straggling civilian garrison settlement which abandoned the name of Maryburgh and adopted the name of Fort William turned out to be a lucky place. For most of the eighteenth century its people made a decent, if occasionally hazardous, living from serving the needs of up to 1,000 soldiers. Early in the peaceful nineteenth century, as the soldiers began to disappear, the Caledonian Canal was opened in 1822, connecting the head of Loch Linnhe by water to the town of Inverness and the east coast of Scotland. The trading benefits of the canal to Fort William were soon augmented by tourism. Southern Victorian products of the Romantic era ventured ever further north beyond the Highland Line, into the once-forbidding badlands. Fort William, which had been established as the region's police station, became its gateway.

According to the *Ordnance Gazetteer of Scotland* of 1882–84, the town was a bustling little place:

It chiefly consists of three parallel lines of buildings, forming two streets [High Street and Low Street], and containing several good hotels and shops, whilst in the suburbs are a number of handsome villas. A favourite tourist resort, and the headquarters of one of the 26 Scottish fishery districts, Fort William has a post office, with money order, savings bank, and telegraph departments, branches of the Bank of Scotland and the British Linen Company and National

Banks, 9 insurance agencies, 6 hotels, a gas company, a public-hall, a new courthouse, a police station, a substantial stone quay (1834), a masonic lodge, a volunteer corps, a hospital founded by Andrew Belford, Esq. of Glenfintaig, for the poor of Kilmallie and Kilmonivaig parishes, and fairs on the forth [*sic*] Wednesday of March, the second Wednesday of June and November, the Tuesday after the second Thursday of July, and the Tuesday fortnight before Falkirk October Tryst.

Trade and tourism in the middle of a relatively healthy crofting and fishing district cemented the fortunes of Fort William. Its economic foundations were well suited to a family of carters and inn-keepers. Allan MacDonald grew up in a comfortable home in a fresh, free and healthy environment. It is an indication of his family's class and aspirations that he was brought up as an accomplished and literate Anglophone, rather than a fluent Gaelic speaker.

'I would give anything if I had been born fifteen miles to the westward [of Fort William],' the adult Allan MacDonald would tell a friend. He meant that in the rural croftlands 15 miles west (or east, or north, or south) of the town he would have been brought up with Gaelic as his first if not only language. His parents, a friend years later would report Allan MacDonald as saying, were 'Highlanders of long descent in Far Lochaber though they were, being innkeepers had the English, and practised it about the house while he was first getting the use of his own tongue. So that the idiom the child of the black house never wastes time learning, that the old folk *salt every sentence with* (as he would say it), he felt he had never fully mastered.'

In fact, despite the fact that his family's quarters in his father's Fort William inns were apparently English-speaking, Allan MacDonald was brought up surrounded by the language. He would write later of the village of his boyhood being 'half lowland and half highland'. But in 1881, the first year in which the British National Census recorded Gaelic speakers, of the 1,600 people who lived in the town of Fort William, no fewer than 1,120 – or 70 per cent – were fluent in the language, as was 85 per cent of the population of the surrounding Lochaber countryside. As Gaelic was not taught to ordinary people in schools at that time, the statistics mean that in 1881 easily three-quarters of Allan's neighbours were native Highlanders.

By that year of 1881, when Allan MacDonald had left the town, its population had risen by a third from the 1,100–1,200 people that he had known as a boy. It is certain that then, back in the 1860s, before the railway line brought people and goods from the south, a higher proportion than 70 per cent of Fort William's people had the native language of the Highlands. The Fort William of Allan MacDonald's childhood was effectively a Gaelic-speaking town, although almost all of its Gaelic-speaking majority would also have been conversant with English.*

The settlement and the district were both still redolent of Gaelic tradition and mythology. As a boy, Allan MacDonald enjoyed wandering by himself along the side of what he knew only as 'the loch' – he would not realise that its full name was Loch Linnhe until he was taught geography at school. Horses were pastured there, on the grassy banks. Although Allan liked and was familiar with horses, he steered well clear of those beasts. One of them might have been the *each uisge*, the water horse of Highland fable: a supernatural creature which could assume the shape of a fine steed but which, if mounted within sight of water, carried its rider to death in the deep loch. 'There was a story the children had,' said Allan, 'of one that let them mount him. His

---

* The rate of decline in Fort William Gaelic between 1881 and 1891, when records were taken, was roughly 5 per cent over the ten years (it accelerated more steeply downhill during the twentieth century). If the same rate of decline can be presumed during the unrecorded decades of the 1860s and 1870s, then the population of Fort William in 1861, when Allan MacDonald was an infant, would have been at least 80 per cent Gaelic-speaking. To put it another way, out of 1,100 people in the town in 1861, it is fair to presume that only about 200 were not Gaelic speakers.

back would be getting longer and longer until they were all on. Then he plunged into the loch, and that was the last of them.'

But English was increasingly the language of commerce, and young Allan MacDonald's family was steeped in commerce. A conscious decision must have been taken – as it would be taken by thousands of other Gaelic parents in the late nineteenth and early twentieth centuries – to educate their children out of the language of the unprofitable, disappearing Highland past, and into the language of the imperial present and glittering future. That decision may have been assisted in the case of John and Margaret MacDonald by the possibility that, while both of their fathers were certainly Gaels, neither John nor John's mother was a native Gaelic speaker.

John MacDonald was, as we have seen, born and brought up in his mother's native parish of Cromdale, Inverallan and Advie, which contained the large new settlement of Grantown-on-Spey. At the time this small district was in eastern Inverness-shire. It would later be absorbed into Morayshire. That transfer was culturally significant. By the nineteenth century most of eastern Inverness-shire was no longer part of the linguistic Gaidhealtachd. In 1881 (the first year that we know for sure) only 27 per cent of the population of Cromdale and Advie combined was Gaelic-speaking, just 22 per cent of the population of Inverallan had the language, as did only 13 per cent of the people of Grantown-on-Spey.

Earlier in the nineteenth century, when John and his mother Elizabeth were raised in Cromdale, Inverallan and Advie, the percentages were probably higher. But they were still not high enough to create a Gaelic-speaking day-to-day environment. When the proportion of Gaelic-speakers in a bilingual community fell below half, Gaelic ceased to be the tongue of regular discourse and its role in that community quickly unravelled. John and Elizabeth MacDonald, baby Allan's father and grandmother, would unavoidably have had some Gaelic words and phrases – nobody in the north of Scotland in their time could practically ignore the language, and their father and husband was a Gaelic speaker. But it is more than likely that the main language of their home and, at least until they moved to Fort William, their neighbourhood, was English.

Margaret MacDonald, Allan's mother, was born and bred further west in Inverness-shire, in the rural Badenoch district of Laggan, and for that reason alone she will have been fluent in Gaelic. In 1881 Laggan was 88 per cent Gaelic-speaking, and when Margaret was a girl in the 1830s there must have been very little else heard on the smallholdings and sheep farms of Laggan.

Margaret's father, Donald MacPherson, was a native Gaelic speaker. Margaret's mother Charlotte's maiden name was MacHardy. She had been born in the Badenoch township of Kingussie in 1787 and was raised there before moving down the strath to marry Donald MacPherson in Laggan. MacHardy was not a common Gaidhealtachd family name, being associated mostly with Banffshire in the north-east of Scotland, which was no longer, in the nineteenth century, a Gaelic-speaking area. But some MacHardys had relocated westward to Kingussie, and Charlotte's childhood there at the end of the eighteenth century would probably have given her complete fluency in Gaelic and would certainly have offered more than a casual acquaintanceship with the language. It is unlikely that Charlotte MacHardy was not a Gaelic speaker, but it is probable that she was completely bilingual, and that her family's default dialect had been Doric, Scots or even English.

She will therefore have been completely comfortable in Gaelic-speaking Laggan early in the nineteenth century. But it is possible that in the privacy of their home her husband deferred to her family's own native language, and that at least one household in Laggan had at times an English-speaking interior.

If those suppositions are correct, it is likely that John Mac-Donald was not brought up with cradle Gaelic from his mother, and had little opportunity to learn it in the fields of Cromdale, Inverallan and Advie. It is equally probable that Margaret MacDonald was totally conversant in the language, but had been raised by a mother who held English in higher esteem.

Margaret MacDonald consequently continued an English-speaking tradition with Allan and her other infants. That would not have stopped every member of both of the generations from having at the very least a useful foundation in Gaelic, and heads full of Gaelic words and phrases. They would be bound to pick some up, from their work and their localities and from the ubiquity of Gaelic in their time. But the fall-back language at their former homes in Inverallan and in Laggan could very well have been English, as it certainly was at Allan MacDonald's childhood home in Fort William.

Allan MacDonald's parents came from households in which Gaelic was very far from being a foreign language, but where, in his words, 'the tradition of Gaelic speech' was broken.

Nonetheless, the grounding in Gaelic given by their environment and by their broad family to Allan and his siblings would relatively easily be lifted into fluency. Allan MacDonald himself was not the only illustration of that fact. His younger brother Ronald left Fort William in his teens to work in Glen Shiel. That rural north-western district was then almost entirely Gaelic-speaking, with a high proportion of people who could speak only Gaelic, and in 1881 the 19-year-old Ronald felt comfortable enough to tell the census enumerator that he also was a Gaelic speaker. If he was not conversant with the language when he left Fort William, Ronald picked up Gaelic extremely quickly in Glen Shiel without the benefit of night school or postal classes. Young Elizabeth, the baby of the family, was 17 at the time of the 1881 census. For reasons which will become clear, Lizzie had by then been living in a fully Gaelic-speaking household for the previous six years. She had fallen into the language with ease. Like her brother Ronald in Glen Shiel, in 1881 the teenaged Lizzie pronounced herself to be a Gaelic speaker.

The MacDonald family might have partly 'given over the use of their mother tongue' but they stayed completely true to their old religion. Allan MacDonald was born into a Roman Catholic family.

2

THE STRANGE LIFE OF
CATHOLIC SCOTLAND

*~ 'That portion of Scotland which has remained
pious and faithful.' ~*

The sixteenth-century Reformation almost destroyed Catholicism in Scotland. If it had not been for the residual strength of the faith in parts of the inaccessible Highlands and Islands, the Scottish Roman Catholic Church would have been reduced to a cypher.

The Protestant fires lit by John Knox in the 1560s laid waste to Catholicism in central and southern Scotland. The penal statutes against the Church of Rome, which were first enacted by the Scottish Parliament in 1560 and were pursued and supplemented in piecemeal form from both Edinburgh and Westminster for a further 233 years, effectively outlawed Catholicism in Scotland. By 1681 it was reported after a four-year survey commissioned by the Sacred Congregation for the Propagation of the Faith that in a total Scottish population of about a million people, only 14,000 were still Catholics.

Of those 14,000 Scottish recusants, the same investigator discovered, no fewer than 12,000 were in the Highlands and Islands. Even allowing for the fact that in 1681 the Scottish Highlands were still relatively well populated in comparison with the rest of the country, that was a remarkable imbalance.

A Morayshire Catholic told Rome seven years later, in 1688, that although there were some 1,200 churches in Scotland, not one of them was Catholic, and 'the severity of the penal laws ... forbid the clergy to celebrate, and the laity to assist at, Mass, under the penal pain of exile, confiscation of property, and death'. There were at the end of the seventeenth century just two Catholic schools in the whole of Scotland, one in the western Highlands in Glengarry, 16 miles north of Fort William, and one in the Hebridean island of Barra.* 'Catholics, in consequence, hold their services in private houses, where sermons are preached and the sacraments are administered: in the Highlands, however, this is done with much greater freedom.'

The Highlands were an exception, though not a complete one: Catholics were still in an overall minority north of the Highland Line. Nor was the survival of the faith purely a product of remoteness. Catholicism remained strong in the southern Outer Hebridean islands, but not in the more distant northern Outer Hebrides of Harris and Lewis, let alone in the ulterior archipelagos of Orkney and Shetland. There were large Catholic communities in western Lochaber and not far to the north in Sutherland and Caithness. The well-populated east-coast counties of Aberdeen and Kincardineshire contained many Catholic redoubts; other less accessible regions did not.

In the Gaelic west Highlands, Catholicism persisted chiefly in a broad arc around the garrison and new town of Fort William.

---

* A few decades later, early in the eighteenth century, a report to the Protestant Society in Scotland for Propagating Christian Knowledge confirmed the continuing existence of the school in Barra and stated that there was also a school in the neighbouring island of 'Southuist ... [where] they are all papists except a very few'. Hearing of these Highland and Island schools, the Sacred Congregation for the Propagation of the Faith in Rome was inclined to propose that Catholic children should be sent to them from all parts of Scotland. Their informant on the ground convinced them that this was impractical, 'assuring the cardinals that Catholic parents in Scotland would as soon send their children to school in Jamaica as to the island of Barra'.

The 30-mile broken coastal strip which ran from Knoydart through Arisaig and Morar to Moidart was largely Catholic, as were the communities inland and to the north of Fort William in Glen Garry, Glen Roy, Glenmoriston and Stratherrick, and to the south in Glencoe and Kinlochleven. There were residual enclaves to the north in villages such as Dornie in Lochalsh and in the glen of Strathglass west of Inverness. The small islands of Eigg and Canna off the Arisaig shore were almost entirely populated by Catholics, as were the distant outer Hebridean islands of Benbecula, South Uist, Eriskay, Barra, Vatersay and Mingulay. Those islands and mainland glens and peninsulas, perceiving themselves as Catholic oases in a desert of Presbyterianism, maintained a fragile confessional as well as linguistic and cultural relationship with one another which would affect the lives of many of their inhabitants. The old religion survived partly where it could not easily be extinguished, partly where it had sunk the strongest roots, and partly on the large estates of sympathetic clan chiefs or other landowners. When a passing bishop was surprised to find a large Catholic community under a Protestant laird in Braemar in the Cairngorm mountains early in the eighteenth century, 'The preservation of the faith through the storms of the Reformation and subsequent revolutions was attributed by the people themselves to the circumstance that the Church had held no possessions there, and that consequently no one had been tempted to make himself master of ecclesiastical property under the pretext of embracing the pure Gospel. More than all, the [Braemar] parish priest at the time of the Reformation, whose name was Owen, had not, like so many others, fled before the tempest, but had remained faithful at his post.' The people of the island of South Uist adhered to Catholicism despite the conversion of their clan chief and landowner to the Protestant communion in the second half of the eighteenth century.

But Braemar and South Uist were exceptions. A priest from Dornie spoke for the broad rule in 1883. When asked why there were Roman Catholics in Arisaig and Morar but not in nearby Glenelg, he replied: 'if the laird was Protestant the people were Protestant, and if the laird was Catholic the people Catholic.'

Those sympathetic clan chiefs would accidentally ensure that what had been a bloody seventeenth century in southern Britain became bloody seventeenth and eighteenth centuries in Scotland, and bad nineteenth and twentieth centuries for Catholics and Protestants alike in the Highlands and Islands of Scotland.

The accession to, or usurpation of, the throne of England, Wales, Ireland and Scotland by William and Mary following the Glorious Revolution of 1688 and 1689 had more devastating consequences in the north-west than anywhere else in the kingdom. Jacobite supporters of the Stuart legitimacy chose to press their claim militarily for the following six decades from safe footholds within the British Isles. The safest footholds geographically were beyond the Highland hills. Those Highland hills also concealed a population of supportive Roman Catholics.

The first Scottish Jacobite Rising took place immediately after the coronation of William and Mary in 1689. It was almost entirely a west Highland revolt involving several Gaelic clans, including the Keppoch MacDonalds. Under the leadership of John Graham of Claverhouse, Viscount Dundee, the forces mustered in Lochaber. While James VII and II re-entered his former kingdom in Catholic Ireland and built an army there, his Scottish Gaelic supporters won a famous victory over superior government forces at the Pass of Killiecrankie in Highland Perthshire. But those original Jacobite rebels lost a third of their complement, including Claverhouse, in the battle, and were defeated at Dunkeld a month later. A year after that, in 1690, James himself was defeated in Ireland by William's army at the Battle of the Boyne. He returned to France, this time for good.

In 1701 James VII and II died in Paris. His son, James Francis Edward Stuart, the man who became known as the 'Old Pretender', assumed the Stuart claim. In 1708 he sailed from

Dunkirk to the Firth of Forth with 6,000 French troops in 30 French ships. They were met there by the Royal Navy and chased anti-clockwise around the north of Scotland before limping back to France, having lost both men and ships but without having put a foot or fired a shot on British soil.

The third rising, in 1715, was launched in the north when James Francis Edward Stuart persuaded the Earl of Mar to muster the Highland clans again. Mar did so, at first with some success, proclaiming James Francis Edward Stuart to be James VIII of Scotland and James III of England and Ireland before marching a sizeable army unsatisfactorily on Stirling and then stuttering to a halt at the demoralising Battle of Sheriffmuir. James Francis Edward Stuart himself arrived in Scotland for the first and last time after Sheriffmuir. He quickly lost faith in his own chances of success and caught a boat back to France early in February 1716. He had spent just six weeks in the country.

In 1719, the French having lost patience with James Francis Edward Stuart, the Old Pretender persuaded Spanish ministers to send 5,000 soldiers on 27 ships to invade England, and two ships with 300 soldiers simultaneously to raise the faithful clans once more in the north-west of Scotland. The larger invasion force was prevented by a storm off Cape Finisterre from getting within 500 miles of the English coast. It went home. The two ships bound for the Scottish Highlands got through. They sailed up Loch Duich, a deep fjord on the Gaelic-speaking west coast, and took the small fortress at Eilean Donan. Augmented by a few hundred Highlanders they then marched 12 miles inland and in upper Glen Shiel were met and defeated, captured and dispersed by an equal-sized but better-organised unit of British Army infantry and dragoons which also included many Highlanders.

After three failed attempts in 11 years the Old Pretender gave up. The consequences of his abortive risings alone on the remnant Scottish Catholic population were severe. There had been in 1704 a rousing Royal Proclamation from William III's sister-in-law and successor, Queen Anne, commanding her subjects to 'put the laws in force against Jesuits, priests, sayers of Mass, resetters or harbourers of priests, or hearers of Mass; to seize and apprehend priests, Papists, and Jesuits; to put down all Mass meetings. All persons who shall apprehend and convict any priest, Papist, traffiquer, Jesuit, harbourer, or resetter, shall have a reward of five hundred merks, besides expenses.'

Despite that re-statement of post-Reformation policy it was generally agreed that Catholicism in Scotland prior to the 1715 Rising in particular (the 1689 revolt was quickly dismissed as just another hot-headed Highland war-party and the small crisis in 1708 could be regarded as an unsuccessful foreign invasion rather than an indigenous insurrection) was 'enjoying peace' and that for the first time in many decades there was 'a lull in the storm of persecution directed against the Catholics … and that many converts were being added to the Church'.

But in the words of a biographer of the Church, 'the first Jacobite rising [of 1715] … entailed fresh sufferings on the Scottish Catholics. Many priests were imprisoned or banished, and from a report of Bishop Gordon sent to Propaganda in 1716, it would seem that the persecution was exceptionally virulent. The Catholics were, indeed, in danger of total annihilation, and it almost appeared as if their religion were on the verge of disappearing from the country.' In 1714 a Catholic seminary was built on the comparative safety of An t-Eilean Ban, a tiny island on Loch Morar on the north-western seaboard. This institution – the first in Scotland since the Reformation 'for the education of Catholic Boys who after trial and preparation there might go to the Scotch Colleges abroad, or, when it should seem proper, might go on with their Studies so as to acquire the learning sufficient for entering into Holy Orders without ever leaving their native Country' – had actually received its founding Master and commenced instruction when the Earl of Mar's rising stuttered to a halt at Sheriffmuir 'and the ensuing Calamities occasioned a dissolution of it …'

But the faith did not 'disappear from the country'. Catholicism lay low in its Highland glens and on its quiet islands and regrouped. In 1731 Rome decided formally to acknowledge the different circumstances of Catholicism in the Lowlands and in the Gaelic Highlands. Catholic Scotland was divided into North and South. The first vicar-apostolic of the North of Scotland – 'the Highland vicariate to include the northern and western districts, together with the islands' – was a 32-year-old Gaelic-speaking native of Morar named Hugh MacDonald.

Hugh MacDonald was still vicar-apostolic of the Highlands and Islands 14 years later, when the big one began.

On 23 July 1745 Charles Edward Stuart, the grandson of the deposed James II and son of James Francis Edward Stuart, landed from a French ship on the white sands of the small Hebridean island of Eriskay, which lay between the staunchly Catholic islands of South Uist and Barra. He was about to become Bonnie Prince Charlie, the Young Pretender.

Among the Highland clans which came out in his support, which marched with Charles as far south as Derby in the English Midlands before doubling back to defeat at Culloden outside Inverness in April 1746, was Clan Donald of Keppoch, the clan of Allan MacDonald's forefathers. The MacDonalds of Keppoch were there from the first raising of Charles Edward Stuart's standard, at Glenfinnan on the western mainland 27 days after he landed on Eriskay, to the crushing defeat at Culloden nine months later. The Keppoch MacDonalds can claim to have started the 1745 Rising before Charles Edward Stuart. Two days before the muster at Glenfinnan, in collaboration with their Lochaber neighbours Clan Cameron, they ambushed, defeated and captured a detachment of British Army soldiers which had been sent to reinforce the garrison at Fort William. The Keppochs went out as they had come in. Shortly before Culloden they attempted to relieve the pressure on the retreating Jacobites by laying siege, unsuccessfully, to the unloved Fort William citadel.

One of the Keppoch MacDonalds, Major Donald MacDonald of Tir na Dris, which is just outside the Lochaber village of Spean Bridge, ten miles north-east of Fort William, was executed at Carlisle in October 1746 for his part in the rising. Donald MacDonald felt obliged to leave behind an apologia which explained that 'I die an unworthy member of the Holy Roman Catholic Church in the Communion in which I have lived . . . And I here declare, upon the faith of a dying man, that it was with no view to establishing that Church or religion in this nation that I joined the Prince, but purely out of duty and allegiance to our only rightful, lawful and native Sovereign, due to him had he been a heathen, Mahommedan or even a Quaker.'

That was both heartfelt and logical, and contained essential truths. Just as there were Highlanders on both sides of the conflict, there were Protestants as well as Catholics throughout Britain who sympathised with and even fought for the cause of Charles Edward Stuart in the middle of the 1740s. His was a dynastic rather than a denominational war. But Donald MacDonald, or any other Catholic clansman, was more than human if he had not hoped that a reversion to the Jacobite from the Hanoverian dynasty would, after two centuries of insult and injury, have redeemed the condition of his Church in Scotland.*

Nor was the Church in the Highlands entirely neutral at the time. The region's vicar-apostolic, Hugh MacDonald of Morar, blessed Charles' standard at Glenfinnan and assigned several

---

* The Stuarts certainly would have sheltered if not restored the Roman Catholic Church. Significantly, there was no mention of Catholicism in the Manifesto proclaimed by 'Prince Regent' Charles Edward Stuart at Glenfinnan on 19 August 1745. It was unnecessary: his family's religious affiliations were taken as read. Instead there was a diplomatic assurance, aimed at most of the rest of the people of Scotland, England and Wales, 'to protect, secure, and maintain all our Protestant subjects in the free exercise of their religion, and in the full enjoyment of all their rights, privileges, and immunities, and in the secure possession of all churches, universities, colleges, and schools . . .' Protestants, Charles was saying, need not fear under his jurisdiction the same penalties that Catholics were enduring in the current order.

of his scarce clergymen as chaplains to the Jacobite army. Hugh MacDonald argued later that he had always disapproved of the 'expedition' and in the August of 1745 had 'counselled [Charles] for the present to return to France'. But 'the prince showed no inclination to follow the advice of the bishop ... and the latter could hardly do otherwise than associate himself with the unanimous action of his people'.

The aftermath of the failed – and final – Jacobite Rising of 1745–46 was unfortunate for Scots of any faith or none, who were for much of the rest of the eighteenth century regarded with suspicion and occasional hostility in the southern regions of the kingdom. It was catastrophic for almost all Highlanders, who bore the brunt of Hanoverian military reprisals, estate confiscations and penal legislation intended to destroy their clannish certainties. The consequent collapse of the clan system of society and land-holding over the next 100 years threw a self-contained, Gaelic-speaking rural people with chivalrous, medieval values onto the Anglophone open market in the high season of unregulated capitalism. They could neither defend themselves nor cope with the trauma. Until the last quarter of the twentieth century the Highlands and Islands would be the only region of Scotland, England and Wales whose population, instead of growing decade after decade, remained in a spiral of perennial decline.

Of course, the Scottish Catholic Church suffered another backlash after 1746. 'The results of the battle of Culloden,' wrote Canon Alphons Bellesheim over a century later, ' ... whatever they may have been for the Scottish people at large, were in the highest degree calamitous to the unfortunate Catholics.'

The small seminary at Scalan, tucked away in the Braes of Glenlivet in south Banffshire, which had been established 30 years earlier in place of the school on Loch Morar which had been scuttled by the 1715 Rising, was torched. William Duthie, the Superior at Scalan in 1746, had seen it coming. 'Mr Duthie had dismissed all the Students to their parents or friends,' recorded another principal of Scalan, Bishop John Geddes, from first-hand recollections shortly afterwards:

> He had also got the sacred vestments and Chalices, the books and even the other moveables carried to the most secret and safe places and this was done with so much prudence that of these things very little was lost. I think it was on the Morning of the 16th of May [1746] that the detachment of the [Hanoverian] Troops surrounded Scalan and orders were immediately given for setting the house on fire nor was it long before these orders were executed. Mr Duthie with a sorrowful heart from one of the neighbouring hills was looking down on the affecting Scene. He saw his habitation surrounded with armed men whom he knew to be then full of barbarous fury; in a short time the smoaky flames began to ascend; he could soon perceive the Roof fall in and after a little there was nothing left but Ruins.
>
> This was to him and to many others a dismal sight, but the worst was that it seemed to be only the beginning of evils; they knew not what was to follow nor where nor when these barbarities were to end; the entire extirpation of the Catholicks out of Scotland was loudly threatened and was justly to have been feared without the interposition of Divine providence in their favour.

Vicar-apostolic Hugh MacDonald, who was an alumnus of both the short-lived seminary on Loch Morar and its carbonised successor at Scalan, prudently fled to Paris in 1746. He would not return until 1749, and for six years thereafter MacDonald ministered to his Highland flocks under the pseudonym 'Mr Brown'. In 1755 the vicar's cover was blown; he was apprehended and put on trial at the High Court in Edinburgh. On 1 March 1756 Hugh MacDonald, having refused to 'purge himself of Popery' was banished for life under pain of death if he returned to Scotland. This time, however, he did not flee abroad. Instead

MacDonald returned to the Highlands and continued to work there until his death from natural causes at the age of 74 in 1773. The authorities in Edinburgh, increasingly weary of civil, confessional strife as the years since Culloden slipped by, and unwilling to create another Catholic martyr, turned a blind eye to the old man's missionary wanderings.

Other priests were imprisoned and detained in warships – one of them an Alexander MacDonald, in the misapprehension that he was actually Hugh MacDonald, the elusive vicar of the Highlands. Displaying a seigneurial insensitivity to British domestic politics, Pope Benedict XIV asked the King of Sardinia, Charles Emmanuel III, to intercede through his London embassy on behalf of the beleaguered Scottish Catholics. Benedict chose Charles Emmanuel because the Sardinian monarch was the great-grandson of the Stuart King Charles I, whose obdurate reign had precipitated a British civil war and who had been executed in London less than 100 years earlier. Charles Emmanuel's intercession had no apparent effect.

In 1747 Pope Benedict made Charles Edward Stuart's younger brother, Henry Benedict Stuart, a cardinal of the Roman Church. Aware of the 22-year-old Henry's dynastic claim in Britain – 'we always considered that after your father James III, and your brother who will be James IV, you will have undoubted right to the English throne' – the Pope inserted a get-out clause into Henry's ordination. 'If hereafter,' said Benedict XIV, 'when you are cardinal-deacon, circumstances should make it advisable, you can resign the hat, marry, and thus avoid destroying the hopes of Ireland, that firm friend of the Stuarts, and of that portion of Scotland which has remained pious and faithful.'

It would never happen. Henry Benedict Stuart died, not as a British monarch but as a cardinal of the Catholic Church, in Rome in 1807. He was interred beside his father, his mother, his older brother and all the serious Jacobite ambitions in the crypt of St Peter's Basilica.

In Scotland the tensions eased slowly. A report to the General Assembly of the Church of Scotland in 1760 commented with something close to resignation on the stubborn survival of Catholicism in the north:

> In countries lying under such complicated disadvantages, it is easy to see the difficulty of extirpating ancient prejudices, and of introducing the Protestant Reformed Religion. The Roman Catholic persuasion, which was formerly established in this and every other part of Great Britain, hath kept possession of many parts of the Highlands ever since the Reformation. Notwithstanding the discouragement given to it at different periods, the zeal of the Church of Rome, together with the concurrence of political causes, hath been hitherto able to preserve and even on some occasions to strengthen that interest.

The Enlightenment law lord Henry Home, Lord Kames, would confirm in 1778 that Scottish Statute Law still required all professors of the Catholic religion to quit the country, while the purchase or dissemination of Catholic books was punishable with banishment and confiscation of personal property. Priests and Jesuits were to be apprehended and punished with death and confiscation, and protecting them was punished with confiscation and banishment, as were hearing Mass, refusing to attend the Protestant service and 'endeavouring to pervert any of his Majesty's subjects, either by reasoning or by books'. Children under the care of Catholic parents or guardians were to be taken from them and placed with Protestant families, and Catholics were not allowed to own land, rule the country or have any official or influential position, which meant they were officially unable to teach.

Not all of those statutes were enforced all of the time. They were by 1778 more honoured in the breach than the observance.

But they hung like Damocles' sword over the heads of Scottish Catholics. 'By the operation of these iniquitous statutes,' said Canon Bellesheim, 'the adherents of the ancient faith in Scotland had been gradually reduced to a condition little better than that of slaves and outlaws.'

Bellesheim was echoing such men as the Anglo-Irish Protestant philosopher-statesman, Edmund Burke, who suggested that the persistent severity of the Penal Laws had ceased by the later eighteenth century to have any purpose other than to prepare British Catholics for perpetuity as an underclass and to justify the Glasgow, Edinburgh and London mobs in their periodical anti-Catholic purges and riots. The Penal Laws, in other words, were no longer necessary, but they were popular. The Protestant constitutional historian Henry Hallam acidly observed 50 years later that 'To have exterminated the Catholics by the sword or expelled them like the Moriscoes of Spain would have been little more repugnant to justice and humanity, but incomparably more politic'.

By 1779 the Jacobite threat had been extinguished and a speaker at the General Assembly of the Church of Scotland estimated the number of Catholics in the country 'at less than 20,000, of whom, according to the same authority, not more than 20 possessed land worth 100 a-year, while in the commercial world there was not one of any eminence'. It was difficult to see what Protestant Scotland stood to fear from such a small minority, however troublesome it might once have been. It was becoming difficult for men of reason and enlightenment to justify their denial of equal citizenship to that minority.

In 1766, following the death of the Old Pretender, James Francis Edward Stuart, the Papacy recognised the Hanoverian dynasty as legitimate monarchs of the British Isles. The domestic quandary was intensified when in 1779 the vicar-apostolic of the Lowlands, George Hay – whose Edinburgh chapel and house had recently been burned by a mob – visited London to present King

George III with a loyal address from Scottish Catholics. Edmund Burke spoke to the parliament at Westminster on their behalf. Burke read out a digest of the Penal Laws still active in Scotland and challenged any other member of the House of Commons to stand and advocate their enforcement. Nobody did so, but parliament moved quietly onto other affairs.

Relief finally came from an unlikely source. The French Revolution of 1789 was anti-clerical, as well as anti-aristocratic. French Catholic priests who fled to London were given an unusually warm welcome by members of the British establishment who suddenly perceived in them many hitherto unsuspected virtues. 'Incredible as such a thing might have seemed a generation before,' mused Canon Bellesheim, 'the exiled and proscribed clergy of France found a hospitable welcome at the hands of the British public, and their immediate wants were supplied by the State.' Their new enemy's enemy became their friend. In 1790 the British Chargé d'Affaires in Paris demanded from the revolutionary administration protection for the Irish and Scots Catholic Colleges in France.

The situation had quickly become absurd. The British Government could not with one hand protest against the persecution of Scottish Catholics in France, while with the other hand suppress Scottish Catholics in Scotland. In the spring of 1793 Robert Dundas, His Majesty's Advocate in Scotland, repealed the more severe Penal Laws, declaring 'the grounds on which the penal statutes had been based to be no longer in existence'. Scottish Catholics still could not vote or become king or queen. They were still excluded from almost all public offices. But their property, heritable rights and comparative freedom of worship were after 1793 guaranteed rather than denied by Scottish law.

Allan MacDonald's grandfather and namesake was an 11-year-old boy in Lochaber when the Penal Laws were first repealed in 1793. He would grow to manhood in times of increasing leniency towards Highland Catholics. He would live to see his children allowed to vote, teach and hold public office. But he cannot have failed to carry with him family memories of the dark centuries which went before.

As the Church in Scotland recovered a form of normality, began to build chapels and subsidise priests, the distinction between its Highland and Lowland branches grew broader. The historian George Chalmers wrote in 1810:

> There still continues in Scotland the remains of the most ancient Church, after all the efforts of reformation, all the harshness of severity, and all the influences of kindness; so difficult is it to eradicate the religious habits of a people . . . These Roman Catholics are generally poor and helpless, quiet and inoffensive, which are qualities that anywhere merit and receive the protection of wise governments.

Chalmers came from Fochabers in Morayshire and was certainly referring to the Highland Catholics of his own experience. West Highland and Hebridean Catholics in particular could with some justification regard themselves not only as the faithful, beating heart of residual Scottish Catholicism, but also as the true embodiment of the 'most ancient' Scottish Church of Columba, Maol Rubha, Moluag and the other Irish Celtic missionary saints.

Ironically – because they also came from Ireland – the immigrant Catholics who would in the nineteenth century resurrect the Church in the Lowlands, and rapidly eclipse in numbers the remnant Highlanders, were not allowed that claim.

The Irish immigrations of the nineteenth century permanently altered the face and focus of Scottish Catholicism. Inside 100 years the Church changed from a small, some thought vanishing, minority clinging to life by its fingertips in pockets of the Hebrides, the western Highlands and Aberdeenshire, to having hundreds of thousands of adherents throughout the industrial central belt. There had been population exchanges between the west of Scotland and the north-east of Ireland for thousands of years. Late in the eighteenth and early in the nineteenth centuries a one-way traffic from west to east across the North Channel began to accelerate, as Irish men and women left their hard-scrabble fields for waged jobs in the industrialised south of Scotland. The Irish famines of the late 1840s and early 1850s increased the surge.

In 1841 44,000 people in Glasgow – 16 per cent of the city's population – had been born in Ireland, and as many as 90,000 Glaswegians were of Irish descent. They were not confined to Glasgow and the west. In Edinburgh and Leith there were in 1800 only about 1,000 Roman Catholics, many of whom were already of Irish or Highland descent. Thirty years later the number of Catholics in the Scottish capital had grown to 14,000, almost all of whom were Irish. In the first third of the nineteenth century alone, new Catholic chapels were raised in Paisley, Dumfries, Dalbeattie, Edinburgh, Glasgow, Greenock and Dundee. In 1851, after the first rush of famine emigrations, over 200,000 people in Scotland – 7 per cent of the entire population of the country – had been born in Ireland, and more than twice that number were of Irish descent.

The incoming Kellys, Murphys, Dochertys, Boyles, Reillys, Gallachers, McLaughlins and O'Donnells were not all Roman Catholics, but most of them were. Within a handful of decades the few thousand indigenous Catholics in the Highlands and Islands went from being the dominant majority of their faith in Scotland to a numerically tiny minority. By 1900 as much as 95 per cent of Scotland's Catholic population was of Irish origin.

The presence of the Catholic Irish was acknowledged by the Church. In 1827 the Highland and Lowland Vicariates were divided into Northern, Eastern and Western Districts. The Highland Vicariate became part of the Western District, which was headquartered in Glasgow. It was far from the end of the Highland

and Hebridean Catholic tradition, but a chain of north-western Gaelic-speaking vicars-apostolic which had run throughout the turbulent eighteenth century was broken. The first vicar of the Western District, from 1827 until his death in 1832, was of Highland descent. He was followed by a succession of men from the south and east.

Allan MacDonald was born and raised in the Western District. He was a fusion of northern mainland Scottish Catholic stock. His paternal grandfather Allan was a Lochaber MacDonald, with all the hereditary ties which that implied. His paternal grandmother Elizabeth came from a central Highland neighbourhood close to the Catholic stronghold of Braemar.

Allan's mother's mother Charlotte was probably from one of the many Catholic enclaves in Aberdeenshire. His mother's father Donald MacPherson was of a Badenoch Catholic family. Between them the four grandparents covered many of the bases, from the western and central Highlands to the cold plains of Aberdeenshire, of vestigial Scottish Catholicism.

The family would find social and religious ease in Fort William in the middle of the nineteenth century. In 1829, when Allan MacDonald's father was a boy, Catholic men throughout Britain were restored to the same limited franchise as common Protestant men – and, in his distant ancestor's words, as heathens, Mahommedans or Quakers. In 1832 a franchise Reform Act ensured that when John MacDonald reached his majority and became a property-holder he would be granted suffrage. As pre-Reformation Highland clansmen did not feature in the medieval Scottish Estates of parliament, John MacDonald would therefore have belonged to the first generation of his family which was allowed to cast a vote for the government of their country. He may have done so, with inscrutable emotions, at one of the three General Elections of the 1850s. Roman Catholic schools were not only tolerated but were allowed government grant aid after 1847.

The long jurisdiction known to Catholics as 'penal Scotland' was over.

They could also worship in peace. Between 1867 and 1868 the Church of the Immaculate Conception, the first Roman Catholic chapel in Fort William, was raised at the south end of the High Street, looking westward over Loch Linnhe. Allan MacDonald was then eight and nine years old. An observant and reverent boy, he would have watched the solid walls of the new church go up and his family would have been among its first communicants. Their pride in that achievement of his Highland co-religionists impressed him deeply and would be echoed by an extraordinary monument in his final parish.

Allan attended in the later 1860s Fort William Roman Catholic School, a small institution which then accommodated a few dozen pupils from the town. Until their integration into the Scottish state system in 1918, such independent Church schools were operated under Canon Law. The faith was the foundation of all instruction. The Catholic Church held that 'religion is the most important subject in education . . . even secular education is not possible in its best form unless religion be made the central, vitalizing, and co-ordinating factor in the life of the child'. All teachers in Catholic schools had of course to subscribe to the Roman Catholic faith, but they were not required to have had educational training. The 'chief manager' or head of the school was invariably a local priest. The great majority of teachers – by about nine to one – were women. If they were nuns they worked without payment. If they were qualified Catholic schoolmistresses their salaries were between half and two-thirds those of their male colleagues. The economic and spiritual imperatives of that situation dictated that most teachers in Catholic schools of the 1860s were female, unpaid or underpaid, and Roman Catholic.

As well as a thorough grounding in his faith, Allan MacDonald was given a solid secular education at Fort William Roman Catholic School. The curriculum offered some promising pupils instruction in Greek, Latin and French and 'domestic economy' for the girls, but put its heaviest emphasis on literacy in English, and numeracy.

Neither Allan MacDonald nor any of his contemporaries were offered any form of education in Gaelic. It is possible that he regretted the omission even as an English-speaking schoolboy. He would write later of his elementary education as being

> ... confined from dawn to dusk in an English school – in a Latin and Greek school if you like – while the language that was most expressive and most natural to me was forbidden. The effect of that is that the twist English put in my mouth then is still there [in adulthood] and will be [throughout my life]. In consequence I will never be completely at ease in Gaelic, and though I hate it with heart and spleen, my Gaelic will always have the harsh, stammering, unpleasant accent of the English speaker which a tongue-tied, limping, stiff-worded English education has left in my head.

The fundamentals of English reading, English writing and arithmetic were in the 1860s and 1870s regarded as essential. The percentage of pupils who had been successfully tested in those three disciplines alone was the benchmark of every Scottish school. Other subjects such as physical geography, botany and physiology were regarded as admirable, but something of a luxury. The result of this narrow but concentrated instruction was that in the 1860s, 89 per cent of all Scottish men and 79 per cent of all Scottish women were able to sign their own names on the marriage register – in other words, were functionally literate. In some sturdy, rural burghs in the Borders and parts of the northeast, literacy reached almost 100 per cent in both genders.

It was a remarkable national achievement, unequalled in Europe outside Germany. But the remote, neglected, sparsely-populated Gaelic-speaking Highlands lagged far behind. When Allan MacDonald was a boy, just 69 per cent of Highland men and less than half of Highland women could write their own names.* John and Margaret MacDonald were determined that their boys and girls would be among the literate. Their use of English at home suggests that it is unlikely that they shared Allan's concern about his lack of Gaelic education.

Allan's comments about being confined in a classroom 'from dawn to dusk' illustrate the fact that school hours were often irregular. Teachers could work shifts from early in the morning to late at night to accommodate a variety of pupils with wildly different needs and curricula. It is possible to picture that busy institution: its Gaelic-speaking students from the outlying croftlands, struggling to master English in their early months in class, reverting instantly to their native language outside the building; its scores of pupils flocking, some shod and some barefoot, through Fort William; its mixture of occasional attendees sporadically released from the potato patch, the hay harvest, the sheep-fank, the cattle byre and the peat-cutting, and diligent day-students from the town's trading classes... and somewhere in among them all a serious, awkward boy with books under his arm, slightly removed from the herd of his contemporaries, punctilious and anxious to be taught, attentively picking up the Gaelic small-talk which surrounded him, but answering only and always in the measured, drawling English of the north-west Highlands.

There we find the 11-year-old Allan MacDonald in the spring of 1871. His 50-year-old father John was by then running the Temperance Hotel at Number 6 on Fort William's High Street, assisted by Allan's 41-year-old mother Margaret and his 17-year-old sister Charlotte, known to all as Lottie. Allan's 13-year-old brother Donald was also at school, as were his nine-year-old brother Ronald and his six-year-old sister Eliza, or Lizzie.

---

* At the same time in England fewer men but more women were literate – 40 per cent and 60 per cent respectively. The claim to superiority within Britain of Scottish education, from the Highlands to the Borders, was chiefly founded on its untypical emphasis on male tuition.

Their priest in Fort William, and therefore the de facto head of the younger MacDonalds' school, was a man of reputation and chequered experience. 'Reverend Coll MacDonald,' said his obituary in the *Catholic Directory* in 1891, 'was born in Lochaber in 1812, and was known throughout the Highlands as Father Coll.'

Father Coll had been ordained in Rome in 1850 and his first mission, at the age of 38, was to the Catholics of the island of Canna. Within 12 months half of the 240 people of Canna had been removed by their landlord, and in June 1851 Father Coll MacDonald was transferred to the nearby western seaboard parish of Knoydart. He had no sooner commenced work in what was then a well-populated district than Knoydart too was cleared. The first 300 emigrants took free passages to Canada in the summer of 1853. Those who had refused to join them were forcibly evicted a few weeks later,

> ... the barns and byres in which they took refuge being pulled down about their ears. During these scenes of violence, Father Coll never ceased to exert himself by every means in his power on behalf of his unfortunate people; and when protest proved unavailing, he took active steps to organise a relief fund in their aid. Many of the emigrants he provided with food and clothing at his own expense; and for those who remained, now destitute and homeless, he procured tents as a temporary shelter, some seven or eight families being thus lodged for some time in his own small garden ... for many years the newly arrived settlers in Canada [from Knoydart], were accustomed to baptize their sons by the familiar name of Coll ...

Another parish having been pulled from under his feet, Coll MacDonald was transferred in 1855 to Fort William, where he would remain in relative security until 1871. In those 16 years he opened the Church of the Immaculate Conception and managed the school before moving back north to Glen Garry, at the other side of Loch Lochy from his birthplace in Glen Roy.

Father Coll was related to the MacKillop family of Glen Roy, a branch of which had earlier emigrated to Australia and produced in 1842 a young woman who, having taken her vows and founded a new congregation of nuns in the Antipodes, sailed to Europe and visited her ancestral Scottish home late in 1873. Sister Mary MacKillop – who would in 2010 become the first Australian to be canonised by the Vatican – spent time with her cousin Father Coll in Fort Augustus and found him to be 'the best and nicest priest I had yet met since I left Rome'.

Part of the function of this decent man with his cellar of dark memories was to identify pupils and parishioners to whom he could recommend the long path towards their own ordination. Few were called, and even fewer either answered or were finally chosen. Father Coll decided that the 11-year-old son of a Fort William innkeeper had sufficient potential. The boy's parents agreed.

Shortly before his twelfth birthday in October 1871, a few months after the 1871 census enumerator had called at the Temperance Hotel, Allan MacDonald took the first step on his priestly vocation. He went away to the other side of Scotland to start the autumn term at Blairs Seminary in what was then Kincardineshire.

3

BLAIRS

~ 'A place where life was ruled unevenly by that ghastly man called Grant.' ~

To an 11-year-old boy from the west Highlands, Blairs was a daunting pile of masonry. It may have been the biggest building that Allan MacDonald had ever seen.

Blairs College was a four-storey country mansion built of unrendered granite blocks. Its front facade alone contained 40 windows, each as tall as a Lochaber crofthouse. The main front doorway was framed by Ionic columns and was big enough to accommodate the Marquess of Breadalbane stagecoach. The college stood in a 1,100-acre estate of home farmland and private woods.

Blairs was a proud achievement of the nineteenth-century Scottish Catholic Church. The troubled, small seminary at Scalan in Glenlivet had been abandoned in 1799 and relocated to Aquhorties, a more substantial country house 30 miles to the east near Inverurie in Aberdeenshire. Four years later in 1803 another seminary was established to serve the west coast, in a comfortable farmhouse on the small offshore Argyllshire island of Lismore. Although several of its mainly Gaelic-speaking alumni went forward to distinguished vocations, Lismore seminary – like

41

its short-lived west Highland predecessors on Loch Morar, at Buorblach by the white sands of Camas Aird nam Fiasgan on the Morar coast, and at Samalaman across the Sound of Arisaig in Moidart – was never able to support more than ten to twenty teenagers at any given time in their rhetoric and grammar classes. Scalan, Samalaman and Lismore had been furtive hedge schools kept alive by heather priests in penal Scotland. In the age of emancipation it was clearly time for Catholic seminaries to re-enter the light of day, as well as time to centralise and expand the preparation of Scottish boys for the priesthood. Blairs came as a gift from heaven.

Or more prosaically, as a gift from the eminent Aberdeen Catholic John Menzies of Pitfodels. Menzies was the last of a landed family line which had fought alongside its west coast Jacobite brethren in the rebellions of 1689, 1715 and 1745, but had somehow managed to retain its extensive properties. At the end of the eighteenth century, in middle age and apparently in terminally bad health, John Menzies sold off all of his inherited estates but Blairs, a serene, secluded vale by the placid River Dee five miles south-west of the city of Aberdeen. He retired there, laid out expansive gardens and contemplated eternity. But the Lord refused to summon John Menzies to His side. In 1827, still alive and thriving at the age of 71, Menzies gifted the Blairs mansion and estate to the Catholic bishops of Scotland. He then moved south to Edinburgh, where he finally went to his reward in his eighty-eighth year in 1843.

St Mary's College at Blairs opened as a Catholic seminary in 1829 with the 25 pupils from Lismore and Aquhorties. Seventy years later, as the nineteenth century turned into the twentieth, Blairs College would be extensively rebuilt and expanded and could in the twentieth century accommodate up to 250 teenaged boys as well as a further 150 priests, nuns and support staff. Throughout the nineteenth century it was a smaller institution. According to the national census taken in the spring of 1871, just a few months before Allan MacDonald arrived at Blairs, there were 49 students at the seminary. They were governed and taught by a rector, a procurator* and three professors, and they were catered to by a dozen laundry maids, kitchen maids, housemaids, serving maids, table maids, a housekeeper and a cook, most of them young women from the surrounding area.

The students ranged in age from 12 to 29 years. Several were in their twenties, but the majority were teenaged. Some of the older students, having determined their vocation, were majoring in divinity and philosophy; most of the younger ones in the arts and grammar.

They came from all over Catholic Scotland and beyond. The variety of his fellow students must have both intimidated and exhilarated Allan MacDonald. They came from the cities of Glasgow, Edinburgh, Dundee and Aberdeen. They came from England and Ireland. Later in his time his fellow students would include one who – in a nice reversal of former circumstances – had fled to Scotland to escape the Franco–Prussian War. Several came from Allan MacDonald's own mainland parish of Kilmonivaig. There were other west Highlanders and islanders: a MacKay from South Uist, a MacDonald from Glenmoriston, a Fraser from Applecross and a pair of MacNeils, aged 12 and 14, from Father Coll MacDonald's former parish in the small island of Canna.

Allan MacDonald was a sensitive man and would have been a delicate boy. He was an intelligent and receptive student, but he did not enjoy his five years at Blairs. The college had a spartan and strictly disciplined regime which was not unusual in nineteenth-century private schools, but which contrasted sharply with his

---

* The 'procurator' was a surviving term for the job which had in some lay universities already been abbreviated to proctor. A procurator had several management duties, the main one being to impose discipline on students. In terms which they will have been expected to understand, he was *in loco parentis* to young men and boys who themselves were *in statu pupillari*.

convivial village and family life on the shore of Loch Linnhe. All
the traditional fasts were firmly enforced, including the 40 days
of Lent, which cannot have helped the concentration of teenaged
boys towards the end of the winter term. The historian, folklorist
and Gaelic-speaking Catholic John Lorne Campbell would write
that 'Fr Allan was heard to say in later life that the training he
received there [at Blairs] had the great advantage of making any
hardships connected with parochial work in the Hebrides seem
luxurious by comparison'.

For the rest of his life Allan MacDonald retained a cordial
dislike of his rector at Blairs College. Reverend Peter Joseph
Grant was in his fiftieth year in 1871. He had been born close to
the shell of the fabled eighteenth-century seminary at Scalan in
Glenlivet, had been one of Blairs' earliest students, had attended
the Scots College in Rome and then returned home to work in
the Catholic mission at Braemar. When young Allan arrived on
Deeside, Peter Joseph Grant had been college rector for seven
years, and would continue in the post for a further nineteen
years. He had a long white beard and a cadaverous, humourless
face which spoke of his chronic ill-health. The college's centenary
history described Rector Grant as 'a man of keen intellect and
deep learning, to which were joined a strength of character and
singleness of purpose'.

None of that is incompatible with the adult Allan MacDonald's
description of his experience of Blairs College as

A place where life was ruled unevenly
By that ghastly man called Grant
Who would make our pens scratch hard
Each Tuesday and Wednesday afternoon
Before he'd put our porridge on the table;
All the same to him were Latin, English,
Or a thousand lines of that monster Homer!

The college prospectus put most emphasis on Latin, the universal

language of the Roman Catholic Church. Ancient Greek –
'that monster Homer!' – was taught, as were French, Italian
and Spanish to young men who could be moving on to the
Catholic Scots Colleges in France, Rome or Valladolid. There
was also 'geography with the use of the globes, philosophy in all
its branches, and divinity'. Allan MacDonald understood the
necessity of Latin, but: 'He had no liking for Greek, which must
have been the fault of his instruction,' a friend would recall, 'nor
for philosophy...'

Gaelic was acknowledged but not taught at Blairs Seminary.
The Church was aware of the size and historical importance of
its Gaelic-speaking congregations, and of the fact that many of
their west-coast priests would be required to serve them. But the
native-cradle Gaelic of those west-coast priests was judged to be
sufficient to the task. In John Lorne Campbell's words: 'Gaelic-
speaking boys were given Fr MacEachen's Gaelic Dictionary and a
copy of the translation of *De Imitatione Christi** and encouraged
to pursue the study of Gaelic in their spare time, such as it was.
This was less training than might be desired, but at the same time
the education given in the study of Latin and Greek trained their
minds to undertake the study of their own language, and many
priests educated in this way, like Fr Allan, learned Gaelic well and
used it effectively.'

Also according to John Lorne Campbell, who was born the
year after Allan MacDonald's death and who lived and studied in
the Catholic Hebrides for two-thirds of the twentieth century,
'one of Fr Allan's teachers [at Blairs] was Fr James A. Smith, later
to be Archbishop of St Andrews and Edinburgh, who noted early
the abilities of his young pupil and encouraged in him an interest

---

* Father Ewen MacEachen was a priest from Arisaig in western Inverness-
shire who had served briefly as a master at the seminary on Lismore. He
published his *Gaelic–English Dictionary* in 1842, and translated both the
New Testament and Thomas à Kempis' The *Imitation of Christ* into his native
language.

in philology and languages which Fr Allan kept up throughout his life'.

James Augustine Smith was a professor at Blairs – one of the three professors in Allan MacDonald's time there – for 23 years, between 1867 and 1890. Blairs employed young priest/professors to work under what must have seemed like the gerontocracy of Rector Grant and his procurator, Andrew Fleming, who was also 50 in 1871. The three professors, James Smith, Donald McIntosh from Braemar and John Paul from Aberdeen, were all in their twenties. Some of their students were older than them. James Smith had been born in Edinburgh in 1841 and was just 29 years old when Allan MacDonald entered Blairs College. Smith's comparative youth and freshness in his post – he had started teaching at Blairs only a year after his own graduation from the Scots College in Rome – undoubtedly made him a more sympathetic figure to the young students than Rector Peter Joseph Grant.

James Smith may have encouraged Allan MacDonald in his study of languages, but as an Edinburgh man he would have been able to offer little more than encouragement in the one language which was becoming MacDonald's consuming interest: Gaelic. Unless Professor Donald McIntosh had absorbed some Upper Deeside Gaelic (which is possible: at least a third of the people of Braemar still spoke it during his boyhood there, and he appears to have had local roots) none of the teachers at Blairs College in the 1870s came from the Scottish Gaidhealtachd. Fortunately, as we have seen, several of the other pupils did. One in particular would become Allan's lifelong friend and colleague.

John Mackintosh was Allan MacDonald's contemporary and countryman, and something of a hero. He had been born at Roy Bridge in the rural Gaidhealtachd of Brae Lochaber in 1859. Mackintosh arrived at Blairs in 1872, the year after Allan MacDonald, so they first met when they were 12 or 13 years old. Unlike Allan, John was a fluent native Gaelic speaker. He was – also unlike the relatively aesthetic Allan MacDonald – a robustly confident gamekeeper's son, a hunter, a stocksman, a fiddler and a natural athlete, with an acute political awareness of what had been done to his people earlier in the nineteenth century that he was never slow to express. Twenty-eight years after they first met, Allan would extol his schoolmate:

He's a hunter in a thousand,
No curlew or heron could escape him,
He would slaughter the mallard
And he was a wearer of sealskins.
In any trade he turned his hand to
He would surpass the professionals –
A fine player of shinty and a cattleman,
He'd be good in a team at any sport.
Skilled at any musical instrument,
The fiddle would sing to his fingers;
He would nurture a toot from a horn
And a blast from the deep throat of a trombone.

This 'clever, breezy' boy's career would run almost parallel to that of Allan MacDonald. They would counterpoise each other. One embodied the heart and the other the head of the late-nineteenth-century Highland Catholic Church. Each recognised, appreciated and envied the other's attributes, and adopted as many of them as humanly possible. John Mackintosh would never make a hunter or a shinty player out of Allan Macdonald, but they shared a facility for song and music. Most crucially to Allan's later work, John – with perhaps the help of a MacKay from South Uist and a MacNeil or two from Canna – could help to give his young friend fluency in Gaelic. At Blairs College in the early 1870s they began that journey together.

Allan MacDonald entered Blairs College as the second son of two prospering parents, and left Deeside as an orphan. His father died at the family's Ben Nevis Hotel in Fort William's High Street on 25 March 1873. John MacDonald's death was recorded by the local GP, Dr David Blair, as having been caused by phthisis and chronic gastritis. That indicates that he had been ill for several weeks, if not months, and died from the untreatable condition now known as pulmonary tuberculosis, and that before killing him the infection had spread from his lungs to his stomach. It was not an unusual nineteenth-century death. John MacDonald was then 53 years old. Allan was 13 and had been away from home for just 20 months.

John MacDonald had put his affairs in order. He left £9.00 to cover his funeral expenses. His furniture and other effects in the Ben Nevis Hotel were worth £175 8s 6d. He had £431 5s 7p saved in the Fort William branch of the National Bank of Scotland and £21 7s 10p in one of the town's other treasuries, the British Linen Company Bank. All told, John MacDonald bequeathed to his widow Margaret, who was left with their young schoolchildren Ronald and Eliza, £637 1s 11p.

It was a substantial amount of money, the equivalent in the early twenty-first century of about £29,000. It was far from being a fortune, but would have given Margaret MacDonald a comfortable pension for her time, if she had lived long enough to enjoy it. She did not. Two and a half years later, on 20 December 1875, Margaret also died. Allan's mother's cause of death was recorded as 'pulmonary congestion (4 days)'. Pulmonary congestion was an accumulation of fluid in the lungs which might occasionally have led to breathlessness, but which in the Highland winter of 1875 quickly caused her heart to fail. She was 45 years old. Allan had passed his sixteenth birthday two months earlier. Both of his parents' death certificates were witnessed by Allan's older brother Donald, who was 15 and 17 years old on the respective occasions.

The brothers and sisters dispersed. Twelve-year-old Lizzie went to live with her uncle Alexander MacIntosh: the same Alexander MacIntosh who 30 years earlier had opened his house at Torlundy to Lizzie's fatherless mother and her widowed grandmother. Alexander was himself a widower in his sixties when he took his young niece into his home at the end of 1875. His automatic familial generosity meant that the girl could continue her schooling in Fort William. After leaving school Lizzie MacDonald joined her older sister Charlotte in domestic service. By 1891 both women were still single (Lottie was then 36 and Lizzie 25) and working as household day servants in Glasgow. They boarded together at the Roman Catholic Chapel House at Rutherglen, south of the River Clyde. The teenaged Ronald moved north and west to work on the home farm of the Shiel Hotel in Glen Shiel in Lochalsh.

Allan MacDonald was advised by his professors and rector at Blairs Seminary to continue his priestly training at one of the Scots Colleges abroad. He applied to and was accepted at the College of San Ambrosio in the northern Spanish city of Valladolid. In September 1876, a month before his seventeenth birthday, Allan travelled over a thousand miles due south from the Highlands of Scotland, into another world.

4

VALLADOLID

~ *'A Scot of Scots, tall, thin, and sinewy, a Highlander,*
a scholar and a linguist, withal a gentleman.' ~

The Scots Colleges in Catholic Europe had been established
during and after the Reformation. The Church's hierarchy
considered that Protestantism had taken hold so quickly and
so surely in Scotland because much of the sixteenth-century
Catholic clergy in that country had been 'ill-prepared, spiritually
and intellectually, for their work'.

More and better seminaries for the training of Scottish priests
were clearly necessary. By the end of the sixteenth century it was
difficult to establish a Catholic hedge school, let alone a fully
fledged college of further education in Scotland itself. Such institutions would have to be set up in continental Europe, where
an older and wiser pastorate could keep an eye on them. In the
second half of the sixteenth century Scots, English and Irish
émigrés crossed the Channel to create their own national colleges
at Douai in northern France, which became for a while 'the chief
centre for those [British Catholics] who were exiled for the Faith'.
In 1600 a Scots College was opened in Rome. The medieval
Collegium Scoticum at the University of Paris became a refuge
for Scottish Catholics, and later a Jacobite training camp.

In 1627 the Scots College in Madrid was opened by a man from Renfrewshire, and the network was complete. The mission statement of the Spanish college was straightforward; the institution was for students:

> Scottish by birth, preferably those of superior character and virtue and those who promise more fruit in the welfare of souls, and they have to spend whatever time may be necessary in studying Grammar and Philosophy, Theology, Controversies and Sacred Scripture, so that when they are well versed in all of these, they may proceed to the said Kingdom of Scotland to preach the Gospel and convert heretics ... when they leave the said seminary for this purpose, others are to be received in their place having the same end, and thus the matter will continue for as long as the aforesaid conversion may require.

For 140 years the seminary led a faltering existence. Its own financial and political problems were not helped by the hapless condition of the Church back in Scotland. The college in Madrid sent no more (and probably fewer) than 17 graduates home to work in the old country between 1627 and 1734, in which year it was effectively abandoned when the nine remaining Scottish students and priests packed themselves and their belongings into four carriages and transferred 800 weary miles north from the capital of Spain to Douai, leaving the building in Madrid in the care and maintenance of a vestigial Spanish staff.

The Scots College in Spain was preserved chiefly by the efforts of Father John Geddes – a Banffshire man, a future Vicar-Apostolic of the Scottish Lowlands and friend of the poet Robert Burns – who reopened it in 1771 in the Jesuit College of San Ambrosio on the outskirts of Valladolid. Geddes was the first rector. He started in northern Spain with fifteen students, including six from Lochaber families and one from South Uist.

Allan MacDonald arrived at this college in the city of the plain a century later, at the end of the summer of 1876. He found both the place and the regime superior to Deeside and Blairs. Why Allan liked the Spanish college is no mystery. It is more difficult to explain how he felt so ardently for Spain.

It was not easy to get further from the north of Scotland than Valladolid and still be in Europe. The climate alone, however prepared for it young Allan was, must have shocked him. In the north of Scotland it was rarely warmer and usually cooler than 20° Centigrade (or as he would have known it, 68° Fahrenheit). In the cloudless summer months on the Old Castilian plateau the mercury routinely hovered between 30° and 40° C (86° to 104° F). Between 80 and 100 inches of rain fell each year on Fort William. There were just 14 to 17 inches of annual precipitation in Valladolid. To put it another way, it rained almost every day in Lochaber, but rain fell on only 70 days out of 365 in that part of northern Spain. Lochaber's climate was maritime, moderate and mild. The weather in Valladolid was described by a Highland priest as 'the excessive cold and moisture of the winter and the blazing scorching sun (worse than Rome) of the summer'.

Allan arrived in this city of 50,000 people in time for the cool autumn and winter months. He acclimatised. Valladolid in the 1870s was proud in its isolation. One of the first Spanish towns to be reclaimed from Moorish occupation 900 years earlier, it had been the capital of Christian Spain until the sixteenth century, a fact which was advertised still by its immense cathedral and abundance of remarkable churches.

Externally the Jesuit College of San Ambrosio was a stern, three-storey eighteenth-century tenement on a wide, open street to the south of the city centre. Its few windows were shuttered and its main arched entrance was barred by two enormous wooden doors. Outside men and donkeys pulled small carts to and from the main market square. Forty years before Allan MacDonald, the Protestant Bible Society agent George Borrow had arrived in Valladolid to discover a brusque and often inhospitable manufacturing town. Hearing from the city's single bookseller that business was so bad that he 'merely carried on bookselling in connexion with other business', Borrow concluded that in the former home town of Miguel de Cervantes 'literature of every description [was] at the lowest ebb'. Borrow paid the 'Scotch College' a visit:

> I found this college, an old gloomy edifice, situated in a retired street. The rector was dressed in the habiliments of a Spanish ecclesiastic, a character which he was evidently anxious of assuming. There was something dry and cold in his manner . . . he was, however, civil and polite, and offered to show me the curiosities of the place. He evidently knew who I was, and on that account was, perhaps, more reserved than he otherwise would have been: not a word passed between us on religious matters . . .

The rector who was reluctant to engage in theological debate with an English Bible Society missionary was an Aberdeenshire man called John Cameron. He had been a student and teacher at Aquhorties, the forerunner to Blairs College, until he was sent to Valladolid at the age of 25 in 1816. Cameron's mood may not have been helped by the fact that Borrow arrived during the first Carlist War, which had helped to reduce the roll at the Scots College in Valladolid to two students, and there were Spanish army officers billeted in San Ambrosio. Rector John Cameron's attachment to the clothing and characteristics 'of a Spanish ecclesiastic' is unsurprising: he spent 60 years there, leaving the country on only one occasion before his death in San Ambrosio College early in 1876, the year of Allan MacDonald's arrival.

The student roll had risen by the year 1876, but Spain was not even then a particularly safe place to be. The second major Carlist War* was under way between 1872 and 1876, and its

---

* Without wandering too far into the Spanish labyrinth: the Carlist Wars of the nineteenth century were conflicts that would have seemed familiar to a Scottish Highlander. Just as the Jacobites had fought for the dynastic claim

shots were heard in the Scots College at Valladolid. The diary of a college professor for Sunday, 4 January 1874, recorded a 'Day of barricades, cannon and musket shot … The *voluntarios* have erected barricades in many parts. Our street … has a barricade at both ends. Firing going on until about six at night, when all is still and quiet as the grave, the forerunner of more mischief. We have prepared the flag in case of need. No bells ringing today. I suppose very few Masses said, at least in public churches.'

Two and a half years later, when Allan MacDonald stepped off the train from Paris and Bordeaux in Valladolid, Spain was once again nominally at peace. Although neither he nor anybody else could confidently have predicted it, the country would remain tranquil for all of his time there.

As Allan arrived in September he would have joined his new colleagues and teachers on their autumn break at Boecillo, the college's country villa. Boecillo was a small pueblo eight miles south of Valladolid. Outside the village, beside the River Duero, the Scots College owned vineyards upon which a previous rector had built a large house with public rooms, quarters for priests and staff, 17 student bedrooms and a dormitory in the attic. The vineyard produced wine which they both drank and sold; the house was used as a rural retreat 'for the health of the lads'.

That quiet, spacious riverside building, with thick earthen walls protecting its pale-skinned inhabitants from the worst of the September heat, must have made a pleasant introduction to Spain. Allan MacDonald found there a companionable group of teenagers and men. There were 17 students at the Scots College

---

in Britain of the descendants of King James VII and II, the Carlists fought for the unrealised claim in Spain of Carlos V and his descendants. Like the Jacobites, the Carlists were ultimately unsuccessful, but – also like the Jacobites – for as long as they campaigned for traditionalism, 'Legitimism and Catholicism' against liberalism, anti-celericalism and republicanism, they enjoyed the broad support of the Church in Spain.

in Valladolid in September 1876, including Allan himself and two other new boys who travelled with him from Scotland. They were mostly in their late teens or early twenties, a few years older than the 16-year-old Allan and a few years closer to ordination. Thirteen of the seventeen were English-speaking Aberdeenshire or Lowland men. The four Gaels, the Highland and Island contingent, consisted of a 23-year-old from Kintail called Duncan MacQueen, a slim and intense 22-year-old from Strathglass called James Chisholm, a sturdy man of the same age from Kilphedar in South Uist called Donald MacLellan and Allan MacDonald himself.

The rector, the Hispanophile John Cameron's successor, was a 67-year-old priest from Fochabers in Morayshire called John Cowie. Like Cameron, Cowie was an alumnus of the short-lived interim seminary at Aquhorties. He had been vice-rector of the Scots College at Rome and a professor at Blairs before becoming John Cameron's vice-rector in Valladolid in 1843. He served under Cameron for 30 years until 1873, when the old man was too weak to carry on and John Cowie became the rector.

John Cowie's stewardship of San Ambrosio was, at its best, dutiful and uninspiring. A teacher of classics, philosophy and latterly theology under John Cameron, he was happy to be an 'unobtrusive' vice-rector. When it became clear in the early 1870s that the rectorship itself would soon be vacant and that he was the heir-apparent, Cowie suffered agonies of self-doubt. They were justified agonies, but he allowed himself to be persuaded by the Scottish bishops to accept the job.

Once in post, his fears about his own fitness for the position manifested themselves in an obsessive scrupulousness. Old John Cameron was still alive and retired in San Ambrosio, which may have contributed to his disciple's insecurities. Cowie clung like a drowning man to the written and unwritten rules of his predecessor. 'Many a time, a concession or permission might reasonably have been granted,' wrote the biographer of the

Spanish colleges Maurice Taylor, 'but was in fact refused, since Cowie had a dread of innovations that might lead to precedents.' When in 1874 and 1875 the new rector instructed the Spanish housekeeper at Boecillo to stop slipping holiday treats to the students and staff, one of Cowie's younger professors openly accused him of 'stinginess' and sighed privately, 'Lord save us from scrupulous Rectors'.

On the last day of December 1875 the students put on a performance of Shakespeare's 'Macbeth' for an audience of their teachers and their peers from the English College in Valladolid. Rector Cowie thought that 'his authority [was] dragged in the mud' by the tunic or gown of the young man playing Lady Macbeth. The next day, apparently considering the previous day's theatrical costume to have represented cross-dressing, Cowie sacked the college tailor and put all the students on extra studies in the evenings. One of his two younger professors threatened to complain to the bishops and resign. John Cowie then revoked the punishment upon receipt of an apology from the students.

The young professor who challenged Cowie was also his vice-rector, and in 1879 – to the relief of the student body – would become his successor. Father David MacDonald was 44 years old in 1876. Like Allan MacDonald, he was a Fort William man who had been educated at Blairs, where he later taught. If David MacDonald needed any further recommendation to Allan, he was also a native Gaelic speaker.

David MacDonald became a professor of classics and philosophy at Valladolid in 1865. He had not particularly wanted to transfer to Spain from his new Glasgow curacy, only accepting the Valladolid posting on an assurance that he could return at will to Scotland. Within weeks of his arrival it seemed that he would soon exercise that get-out clause. 'Neither the college in town nor the villa are any great shakes...' he wrote back to Scotland. 'I certainly cannot say I am pleased with my change or that I am at all happy here.' In the event, David MacDonald would stay at the Scots College in Valladolid for the rest of his life, a further 44 years; 'Don David', as he came to be known, would, like Rector John Cameron, retire and die there.

Father David MacDonald was 'strong-willed, energetic, versatile, a natural leader; in physical appearance, tall, large-framed, rather gaunt'. He was 'a Scot of Scots, tall, thin, and sinewy, a Highlander, a scholar and a linguist, withal a gentleman'. He was 'opposed to all hypocrisy and pretence, with a complete lack of tact'. David MacDonald was self-confident, opinionated and pugnacious. He disliked the Cameron regime when he arrived in 1865, and he disliked even more the Cowie regime which succeeded it in 1873. As he did not hesitate to express his disapproval of the college seniors to any Scottish bishop who would listen, it is reasonable to suppose that students such as Allan MacDonald also got a glimpse of their young professor's thrilling iconoclasm. David MacDonald did not have the tact to hide his feelings from them. 'David MacDonald,' it would be said, 'probably regarded "tact" as another word for hypocrisy.' He may have been a youngish Turk, but it would be wrong to picture Father David as a soft-hearted liberal rebelling against the strictures of his elders. David MacDonald was able to offer his students some leeway, in their academic and personal lives, simply because he was more certain of himself than John Cowie had been. His confidence commanded respect. He loved the open air and manly exercise, especially swimming, which was guaranteed to endear him to young men. He also believed that teenagers at least were in regular need of what he called 'skelps and cane-ology'.

Allan MacDonald had Father David as one of his teachers for his first two years at San Ambrosio, and as the college's rector for his last four years. David MacDonald was undoubtedly, as John Lorne Campbell would say, 'the main influence' on Allan's student life in Spain. As such, Father David must take credit for the fact that his younger clansman thrived there.

Allan MacDonald's days and nights, months and years at San

Ambrosio were circumscribed by an established timetable. The students rose at 6.00 a.m. in the winter months, and at 5.00 a.m. between Easter and September. They then had half an hour to wash and dress and make their beds, followed by an hour of prayer, meditation and spiritual reading before Mass. There was an hour's study after Mass and before their breakfast of gazpacho and milk, eggs and fruit when available. It would then be 10.00 a.m. in the winter and 9.00 a.m. in the summer. They would take classes until 12.45 p.m., then say the rosary before dinner at 1.00 p.m. This midday meal was plentiful. A thick soup or stew was followed by roast beef, pork, sausages, fish or omelette and then by cheese or fruit. After dinner there would be a period of digestion and recreation, and at 3.00 p.m. on most afternoons they would recommence classes, which continued until 7.30 p.m. Occasionally an orderly, chaperoned walk into the town or surrounding countryside would be substituted for some or all of the afternoon classes. At 7.30 the litany and lives of the saints were recited. At 8.00 p.m. they had supper, which was a gentler reprise of dinner without the first course of stew or soup. There were prayers at 9.00 p.m. and lights out 30 minutes later.

For a fortnight between Easter and Pentecost and during almost the whole of September and October, when the entire college decamped to the villa at Boecillo, Allan and his colleagues were allowed to lie in bed until 6.30 a.m. There were no classes and only two hours' daily study. They could by Allan MacDonald's time there take donkey excursions, swim in the River Duero and play games of cricket on the threshing ground. After breakfast and dinner they were obliged to take long walks, on the understanding that they did not 'go into villages nor cross rivers, nor remove from the house further than a league ... [nor] purchase wine, spirits, milk, eatables or any such thing, nor accept of them if offered ... [nor] carry grapes nor any kind of fruit to the house'.

The detail of the restrictions indicates that lively young men occasionally transgressed. The college was haunted by intermittent scandals, which rectors Cameron, Cowie and later David MacDonald were all anxious to avoid. In 1860 one of the most promising students had left, apparently to return to Scotland. It was later discovered that he had travelled no further than Santander on the Basque coast of northern Spain, where he was met by and instantly married to one of the college maids. In 1865 Rector John Cameron found himself having to confiscate an unsuitable book – the comedies of Aristophanes – from a new student.

Some diversions were allowed. They had ten days off classes around Christmas, when they were allowed to go skating on frozen mill ponds or canals. Feast days were celebrated. David MacDonald, who was then vice-rector, described in his diary the festivities of St Margaret's Day at the Scots College in Valladolid in November 1875: 'Day sunny but cool. High Mass at 8¼. English students over [from the English Catholic College]. At dinner the usual company. Began with slices of orange. Then two kinds of soup, *puchero (garbanzos – verdura – tocino – jamon – salchichas – breadstuff – pollo – carne*); then a dish of ham, eggs and green peas – partridges – salmon – veal and salad – *flan* and another pudding – *orejadas – guindas* and apricots – etc. After dinner coffee and sweets in Mr Cameron's room. The company departed around three o'clock.' Allowing even for the fact that St Margaret is a patron saint of Scotland, the scholars and their superiors could eat well.

They enjoyed the recreations of any respectable group of late-Victorian British students. They occasionally held tea-nights: 'a special tea with cakes and sweet things, followed by a social evening of songs, wine, sometimes speeches and toasts, and finally cards'. They played energetic British and Spanish parlour games. Under the auspices of the maligned Rector Cowie in 1874 a handwritten college magazine, 'The Academician', was founded, and shortly afterwards the student dramatic performances, whose costumes would later give the rector such trouble, were allowed.

Cowie also revived the college's weekly Academy, where students declaimed essays and original speeches or lectures to one another. The popular Academy was another nod to their host country. 'For is it not in preaching especially that Spaniards hold the preeminence above their brother priests in Scotland?' Father David asked his diary rhetorically. 'We have the means in our Academy of becoming good preachers and doing honour to our Alma Mater.'*

Allan MacDonald was happy and healthy in Valladolid. There is a photograph of him in a posed group of fellow students in San Ambrosio. It was taken in 1878 or 1879, when Allan was probably either 18 or 19 years old. He is among the youngest of the group of 12: all the others but one are in their early twenties. They are wearing Spanish birettas on their heads and white becas – the Spanish collegian's sashes – are folded over the chest and shoulders of their black college gowns. (They are in fact, as George Borrow had noted 40 years earlier, 'dressed in the habiliments of a Spanish ecclesiastic'.) Allan looks contented and hearty. It is evident that he was, in his late teens, already fast approaching his full impressive height: the 6' 3" of his maturity. But in the photograph he is well built, his young face is rounded and full, his eyes have the intelligent, humorous sparkle that they at least would never lose. His jaw is firm, his head is set askance and he gazes almost jauntily at the camera. It is the face of the young man who would fondly remember, two decades later,

> We spent a while in Spain together,
> A place of no small happiness to us,
> And we plucked the grape of wine

---

* It might have worked. In 2009 a Hebridean priest, Father Michael MacDonald of Bornish in South Uist, would write: 'The College in Spain had a reputation, at least by its own account, of producing great preachers. This may in fact have been true. I remember my grandmother having a saying [about the continental Scots Colleges]: "France is for the worker; Spain is for the preacher; and Rome is for the learned man."'

And quenched our appetite with oranges
There's no doubt but that we grew
In sharpness of mind as was proper for us . . .

In 1880 Allan MacDonald's Spanish life was made almost complete. He was joined in Valladolid by his friend from Blairs College and fellow Abrach (person from Lochaber), John Mackintosh. John had travelled around since leaving Blairs in 1877, the year after Allan. He had gone first to the Scots College at Douai in northern France. A year later, in 1878, John moved south to the Saint Sulpice seminary at Issy-les-Moulineaux on the outskirts of Paris. He was reunited with Allan MacDonald at the Scots College in Valladolid in November 1880.

Allan's pleasure at the reunion was increased by the fact that John Mackintosh gave him another Gaelic speaker to practise on. Donald MacLellan from South Uist had returned in poor health to Scotland in the June of 1880. The appearance of John Mackintosh at Valladolid pushed the college's Gaelic-speaking complement back up to four, including the other students James Chisholm and Duncan MacQueen and of course the new rector, David MacDonald, who had been appointed to the top job after the death of John Cowie in March 1879.

Where rectors Cameron and Cowie had been at best indifferent to Gaelic, David MacDonald encouraged his students both to practise and to learn the language. That was not only because Gaelic was Father David's own native tongue, or because he was 'a Highlander, a scholar and a linguist'. It was also because he had a west-coast Highlander's real understanding of the fact that many of his students would be sent to serve Catholic communities in which every single communicant spoke Gaelic as their first language, and many of the congregation neither spoke nor understood any other language.

That had been the case for centuries. It was given additional emphasis in 1878, following the death of the last vicar of the north, Bishop James Francis Kyle, by the restoration of the Roman Catholic hierarchy in Scotland and the creation of a new diocese which contained all of those traditional Gaelic-speaking Catholic districts.*

The first Bishop of Argyll and the Isles was beginning his duties at his new See in Oban as Allan MacDonald studied in Valladolid. Bishop Angus MacDonald was yet another Gaelic-speaking western Highlander. He had been born into a relatively affluent landed family in the lonely Moidart enclave of Glenaladale in 1844 and was only 34 years old when he was taken from his curacy at Arisaig and given the new diocese. Perhaps the pope and the Scottish hierarchy realised the energy and physical effort that would be required of their bishop in that expanse of archipelagos and mountains. If so, they had found the man for the job. He would be eulogised,

> The Right Rev. Angus Macdonald as Bishop of Argyle and the Isles, had within his See all the [old Highland and Island Roman Catholic] districts . . . and in almost every one of them he left the impress of his character. New churches arose under his influence, new missions were opened, and a spirit of fervour was enkindled in priests and people alike, which was very remarkable.
>
> Endless were the journeyings by sea and by land which the Bishop performed in the visitation of his flock. From mainland to island, from town to hamlet he went, serving his people, preaching to them and confirming them, in winter as in summer, in fair weather as in foul. A man of greater physical strength might easily have felt in fewer years the strain of such manifold activities.

---

* The reconstituted Catholic hierarchy in Scotland replaced the three vicariates of the Northern, Western and Eastern Districts with two archbishoprics, at St Andrews-with-Edinburgh and at Glasgow, and four bishoprics: at Aberdeen, Dunkeld, Galloway, and what could be termed the Gaelic diocese of Argyll and the Isles.

Few people were better qualified than Angus MacDonald to understand the importance of Gaelic in the Catholic communities of the Diocese of Argyll and the Isles. There were plenty of Gaels in the north-western Highlands and Islands who were not Roman Catholics. But there was hardly a single Catholic in the Scottish Gaidhealtachd who was not a Gaelic speaker. Bishop Angus MacDonald maintained a regular correspondence with his fellow West Coast Gael, Rector David MacDonald of the Scots College in Valladolid. It is not a coincidence that four of the five Gaelic-speaking students in Allan MacDonald's generation at Valladolid would eventually be directed to a Gaelic-speaking community by the first Bishop of Argyll and the Isles. Donald MacLellan from South Uist would recover from illness and work on the western mainland in Morar. James Chisholm from Strathglass would go to the island of Barra. John Mackintosh would spend almost 20 years in South Uist. The learner in their midst, Allan MacDonald, would proceed to live, work and die in the islands of the southern Outer Hebrides.*

There was therefore from 1878 onwards a vocational purpose to Allan MacDonald's pursuit of fluency in the 'mother tongue' which his parents had 'given over'. In every other way he was a north-west Highlander to his core. He cannot have visualised an ideal future outside the Diocese of Argyll and the Isles. But without fluent Gaelic he could not realistically expect to be posted to such heartlands as Arisaig or the Hebrides. Without Gaelic his future was more likely to lie in some benighted Glasgow parish or among the John Cowies and Peter Grants of the dour north-east. With Gaelic, the hills and the islands of his people beckoned him. Luckily, with three fellow students and a supportive rector

---

* The fifth Valladolid Gael of Allan MacDonald's student years, Duncan MacQueen from Kintail, worked for almost 30 years in Inverness at the end of the nineteenth and beginning of the twentieth centuries. His Gaelic would still have been useful there, not least among the economic migrants to the town from the west coast and the islands.

to whom the use of Gaelic was as natural as breathing, Allan MacDonald was able to create for himself at the Scots College in Valladolid a form of Gaelic immersion course. He was anxious to achieve literacy in the language as well as verbal fluency. A shortage of devotional and secular Gaelic literature cannot have made that easy. At that time and for decades afterwards, most native Gaelic speakers had difficulty in writing and even reading their language. It was not uncommon to find an educated Gael who spoke perfect Gaelic but who, thanks to the Anglophone education system, could read and write only English. The private correspondence between Rector David MacDonald and Bishop Angus MacDonald, both of whom were probably most comfortable conversing in their western seaboard Gaelic, was conducted entirely in English. The injustice of that situation was never lost on Allan MacDonald. He would devote much of his life to trying to improve it. For the moment, in Valladolid in the late 1870s and early 1880s, he strained towards literacy by writing poetry – that most accommodating of literary forms – in Gaelic.

Linguistics were not the only intellectual recreation at San Ambrosio and Boecello. Nineteenth-century European Christian churches of all denominations, facing unprecedented social and political forces, were alive with theories and competing dogma. Most of it was and remained irrelevant and largely incomprehensible to the lay communities, whatever their native language. But Allan MacDonald was a student of theology. He will have sat up and paid attention when the other professor at Valladolid returned from a visit to the north one day bubbling over with Thomism – or more accurately, Neothomism.

The other professor was a man from Inverness called James MacDonald. He went to Valladolid as a 35 year-old in 1875 to assist David MacDonald under John Cowie's rectorship. By the time of Cowie's death in 1879, and the promotion of David MacDonald to the rectorship, the college's roll had reduced sufficiently for the Scottish bishops to agree that the two relatively young men could handle the teaching duties between them. From 1878 until Allan MacDonald left Valladolid, David MacDonald and James MacDonald, rector and vice-rector respectively, were his only adult teachers. To avoid the confusion of two Father MacDonalds, they became familiarly known as Father David and Father James. The latter's Neothomism offers a view of the debates and tensions which fermented in such small seminaries of the time.

Father James rediscovered the thirteenth-century philosophy of St Thomas Aquinas at about the same time as Pope Leo XIII, who in 1879 attempted to provoke a revival of Aquinas' 'Thomistic' doctrines. Thomism fell nicely into the curriculum of institutions which focused on the study of both theology and philosophy. Aquinas had rarely fallen out of favour in the Spanish Church. He was especially popular among the teaching Jesuits in Iberia. The apparent down-to-earth empiricism of Thomism also made it perennially acceptable to Britons, particularly to post-Enlightenment Scottish Britons. So it should have come as no surprise when at the end of October 1880 Allan MacDonald and the other students returned to Valladolid from their autumn break at the Boecillo villa to be met by a 'Thomistic and pugnacious' Father James, who had spent his autumn break in Scotland.

'That little firebrand came back,' wrote Rector David Mac-Donald to Bishop Angus MacDonald in Oban, 'setting us all at loggerheads with questions about the *"Haecceitas"* of something, matter and form etc., until we have threatened to silence him by an *argumentum a posteriori*.'

Father David and Father James disagreed about several things. Father James hated the student theatricals which Father David continued to tolerate if not encourage. Father James thought the students guilty of 'frivolous and vulgar habits' such as giving each other nicknames. Once Father James had left for Innerleithen in 1886, Father David approved the purchase and installation of a billiards table in the college. But for as long as they were at

Valladolid together, the two men were interdependent. Father David might express to Bishop Angus his exasperation with Father James' aggressive Neothomism – as if nobody else, even the college rector, had ever read Thomas Aquinas, or heard of the *'Haecceitas'* principle of John Duns Scotus! But he would quickly calm down and remind himself and anybody else that James MacDonald was 'a real treasure to the College for his assiduity and success in teaching and profound piety'. There was still a sense of embattlement in the Highland Catholic Church, even in Valladolid in the 1880s. They needed one another.

In March 1882, after five and a half years of grapes, oranges, prayer and study in Spain, Allan MacDonald returned to Scotland. He was 22 years old.

5

OBAN

~ *'The capital of the West Highlands and the Charing Cross of the Hebrides.'* ~

He was ordained a priest by the new Archbishop of Glasgow, Charles Eyre, in that city in July 1882. His examiners in Scotland reported to Archbishop Eyre that they were 'very well satisfied' with Allan MacDonald, 'not only with his theoretical knowledge, but also with the prudence and good sense with which he applies this knowledge to particular cases'. He was, in the words of his former rector David MacDonald, 'without any canonical impediment, except want of age'.

Allan MacDonald was then sent north not to be assigned a Highland parish of his own but to work under the Bishop of Argyll and the Isles, Angus MacDonald, in the Cathedral parish at Oban.

There were two probable reasons behind that mildly disappointing posting. Allan's fluency in Gaelic might have been judged by Rector David MacDonald in Valladolid to be as yet inadequate for a native Gaelic-speaking congregation. Occasional immersion with a handful of Gaels in Spain would have been no substitute for daily intercourse with ordinary Highlanders who spoke hardly anything but Gaelic. If that was the case, if Allan MacDonald's

Gaelic was not yet up to scratch in 1882, Father David would certainly have appraised his correspondent and contemporary, Bishop Angus MacDonald, of the fact.

It is also true that, despite his favourable reports, Allan MacDonald was not yet so far up the priestly pyramid as some of his fellow students. In November 1881 the college in Valladolid had been visited by Bishop Joseph Benedict Serra of Perth in Australia, an elderly Spanish cleric who had come home from the Antipodes. While at San Ambrosio – which was not often honoured by the presence of bishops from any country – Bishop Serra was asked by Rector David MacDonald to raise most of his senior students to the subdiaconate, to make them sub-deacons, the first and lowest rung on the vocational ladder. James Chisholm was elevated in the college chapel, as was Duncan MacQueen and Allan's exact contemporary John Mackintosh. Allan MacDonald himself was the only student of his generation not to be made a sub-deacon in 1881 by Bishop Serra.

His two years in Oban between 1882 and 1884 would have been good for his Gaelic and gentle in their demands on the young priest. The 22-year-old Father Allan was working under another Lochaber Gaelic speaker. He was also working in a town with hardly any Roman Catholics but a lot of Gaels. Estimates of the number of Catholics in Oban itself in the early 1880s vary between one family and four families. It has been said that in his first years there Bishop Angus MacDonald needed a bodyguard to walk around the town.* One of the Catholic families in Oban during Allan MacDonald's time there was that of a fisherman named Donald MacLeod, from the small island of Eigg. Donald MacLeod gave to the young priest some traditional Gaelic hymns

---

* The size of the small Catholic minority in Oban at that time can best be gauged by the school rolls. Oban High School had in the early 1880s an average attendance of 268 children, Oban Episcopalian School had 88 pupils, and the new Oban Roman Catholic School had just 24 regulars.

and probably other nuggets of Hebridean folklore. The fisherman from Eigg played therefore an important part in the early development of a remarkable calling.

More than half of the 4,000 Protestant fisherfolk and tradespeople in Oban were Gaelic speakers, and in the surrounding rural crofting area of South Lorn, 90 per cent of the people were fluent native Gaels. The inhabited offshore islands, such as Kerrera and Lismore, were as close to totally Gaelic-speaking as made no difference. The new Cathedral of Argyll and the Isles might not have given Father Allan much practice in his priestly vocation, but with a bit of application it will have done wonders for his Gaelic.

The See had not been established in Oban in 1878 because of its numbers of Catholics or Gaelic speakers. The Diocese of Argyll and the Isles was centred there largely because Oban was at that time, in the words of the *Ordnance Gazetteer of Scotland* which was published in 1882, 'the capital of the West Highlands and the Charing Cross of the Hebrides'.

> Oban is the focus of steam communication, by land and sea, between the south and the north-western parts of Scotland. It is the terminus of an important railway line, affording direct communication with Edinburgh and Glasgow; it is the final point of the so-called 'royal route' from Glasgow via the Crinan Canal, carried on in the splendid steamers *Columba* and *Iona*; it is an important port of call for the larger steamers *Claymore* and *Clansman*, after they have 'rounded the Mull' of Kintyre on their voyage from Glasgow to Stornoway; it is the starting place for numerous steamer-routes throughout all the western coast and islands ...

From this Charing Cross of the Hebrides, Bishop MacDonald could most easily visit the furthermost peripheries of his north-western Catholic community, while living within a train journey of the archbishoprics of Glasgow and Edinburgh.

Oban was also the mainland town closest to the sacred island of Iona, where Columba had established his Gaelic Christian mission to Scotland 1,300 years earlier. Bishop MacDonald raised in 1878 and 1879 a temporary Cathedral of St Columba on the Oban sea-front. It was made of wood and corrugated iron and had seats for 300 worshippers. (Oban Parish Church seated 500, St Columba's Established Church held 600, the Scottish Episcopal Church of St John the Evangelist had 400 sittings, and the town had also a large Free Church, a United Presbyterian Church and a Congregational Church.) The first St Columba's Cathedral was supposed to be an intermediate structure. It lasted for 50 years.

Father Allan MacDonald was back home. He might not yet have his own parish, but he was in a beautiful west Highland town in exciting times. This large, fit, healthy young man strode energetically around a new jerry-built cathedral and a new small school. He walked up and down the breezy, busy esplanade. He felt the Highland winds grow warmer as the spring days lengthened. He felt the pulse of Oban quicken as,

> . . . by the end of June it awakens to a hurried, brisk, active existence, which lasts for the rest of the summer and autumn. When the tourist season once begins, Oban is bustling and gay. Train and steamer and coach pour streams of eager pleasure-seekers into the town – all countries of the world are represented, all ages and ranks in its hotels and streets. The shriek of the engines, the clear tones of the steamer bells, and the rumble of wheels are heard more frequently; the hotels hoist their flags; bands play on the promenade; graceful white-sailed yachts glide into the bay and drop anchor; tourists and canvas-shoed yachtsmen throng the streets and shops; and there is a general air of bustle and of coming and going.

As well as its seven churches, Oban had a newly opened library and public reading-room, a Scientific and Literary Association, an agricultural society, a Volunteer Improvement Association, the headquarters of the Royal Highland Yacht Club, two weekly newspapers, cattle, horse and sheep and wool markets, and more hotels per head of population than Edinburgh.

All this cheerful commerce could not mask the fact that Allan MacDonald returned to the Highlands at a time of political and social unrest. In 1883 a Royal Commission chaired by the ninth Lord Napier was touring the Highlands and Islands taking evidence from land-hungry crofters and cottars, from estate factors and owners, from ministers, priests, schoolteachers and almost anybody else with an interest in the Highland land struggle. Allan MacDonald will have followed the hearings of the Napier Commission closely, partly because some people he knew –one of whom, Father Sandy Mackintosh of Daliburgh in South Uist, was a family relative – testified to it, partly because local and national newspapers such as the *Oban Times* and the *Scotsman* reported on it comprehensively, but chiefly because everybody in the Highlands and Islands was absorbed by the commission and its hearings. In 1883 Lord Napier headed the biggest show in town.

So Father Allan will have read with fascination the testimony of his fellow San Ambrosian James Chisholm from Strathglass. The newly ordained James had been sent in 1882 straight from Valladolid to what might have been Allan MacDonald's own dream parish: the Outer Hebridean island of Barra, where 1,900 of the 2,000 people were Gaelic speakers, 1,000 of them spoke no other language and 95 per cent of the population was Roman Catholic. When the Napier Commission set up its stand in Castlebay in Barra in May 1883, the 29-year-old Father James Chisholm took the opportunity to air a longstanding local grievance. 'We in Barra here,' said the young priest, 'are almost entirely Catholics, and still we have to submit to seeing our children taught by teachers who do not belong to our own denomination.'

The problem was not only in Barra but in all of the Catholic islands owned by the Gordon Cathcart estate: Mingulay, Vatersay, Barra, Eriskay, South Uist and Benbecula. The elected School Boards which employed teachers in those islands had a traditionally inbuilt Protestant majority, which was promoted and protected by the Protestant estate management and its tenant farmers. In effect, the devotional balance of power on the School Boards, and consequently in the schools themselves, was gerrymandered by the Protestant minority. At a time of clearances and land wars, suggested James Chisholm, the usual democratic corrective did not apply in the Hebrides: 'Yes, at [the] next election we can rectify the matter; but we are more or less afraid of appealing to the people, because they might be affected by superior influence, owing to the factor not belonging to that [Catholic] denomination.'

Seven days before Father James Chisholm addressed the Napier Commission in May 1883, Bishop Angus MacDonald sat down in the Oban Priest's House which he shared with Father Allan MacDonald and wrote to the Napier Commission on the same subject.

I refer to the way in which the Catholics (ie, the great bulk of the population) of South Uist and Barra have been dealt with in educational matters, in being refused Catholic teachers in schools attended almost exclusively by Catholic children . . .

I believe that a statement of this case will tend to show the existence of a widespread evil, in the dependant and degrading position in which such tenants are apt to be placed – with no security of tenure, no guarantee against removal at will, and with the fear constantly hanging over them, that if they venture to assert their rights they may be made to suffer for it, without having power to obtain redress . . . In other Catholic districts on the mainland, Catholics had their feelings invariably respected by [school] boards composed mainly of non-Catholic members. Here [in the islands], where they could have by their votes secured a majority of seats and then looked after their own interests, they were deterred by fear from exercising that right.*

Bishop MacDonald was determined, he wrote, 'to obtain redress for the people'. His young priests took note of that determination.

John Mackintosh left Valladolid five months after Allan MacDonald. He was ordained a priest in the college chapel at San Ambrosio and returned to Scotland in August 1882. The following year, while Allan was still in Oban, Father John was despatched by Bishop Angus MacDonald to join James Chisholm in the Outer Hebrides. John Mackintosh was given the parish of Bornish, a busy crofting community in the middle of the island of South Uist.

Twelve months later, in 1884, Father Allan MacDonald's vocational skills and command of Gaelic were judged adequate enough for him to join his two college friends. He was offered a teaching post at Blairs College, but the large parish of Daliburgh at the south end of South Uist became vacant. There was no serious choice to be made. At the age of 24 years, Allan MacDonald crossed the Minch for good.

---

* The Protestant minority replied that no Catholic needed to worry about being evicted for voting against the factor's interests, that teaching in the board schools was non-denominational if not secular, and that the Protestant churches had done more for education in the islands than the Catholics.

6

SOUTH UIST

*~ 'The Uist people are born gentlemen – Nature's
noblemen.' ~*

The generation of mainland men who became island priests in the
early 1880s made a template for their successors throughout the
twentieth century.

They were self-conscious representatives of the Old Religion.
The Gaelic identity which they embraced and cultivated was
part of a millennial connection to the original Celtic Church.
They perceived themselves as the heritors of a Christian faith
which had lived in the Highlands before the Free Church, the
Episcopalian Church or the Established Church of Scotland.
Their Church had not only been around for 1,000 years before
the Reformation; it predated in Scotland the Catholicism of the
nineteenth-century immigrants. There were conflicts of identity
in the south of Scotland between the few remaining native
Scottish Catholics and the hundreds of thousands of incoming
Catholics from Ireland. There were no such tensions in Barra
and South Uist. In those north-western fastnesses Catholicism
seemed never to have lost its way. It had remained the main, if
not the only, indigenous faith without interruption from the
Dark Age conversions made by St Columba and others, through

the Reformation and through the subsequent centuries of penal Scotland. If there was a true, eternal Church anywhere in the realm, those young priests were assured, they were its clergy and their people its followers. They felt themselves to be, if not independent, slightly apart from the hierarchies of Britain and Rome. That distinction, that uniqueness, was as much a product of history, language and culture as of geography. It anchored them in their Hebridean islands; it gave them a security and even a boldness which Catholic priests elsewhere in Britain were not always able to share.

They were aware of the honour and responsibilities which were laid upon them in being sent to serve such loyal, insular congregations. It was as if they had been given the care of a small light which had never gone out. If they were not strong and articulate when they arrived in the Hebrides, they gathered strength and learned to speak. They became builders. They were among the first priests who were able to build in Scotland since the sixteenth century, and there was a lot of building and rebuilding to be done in the most impoverished diocese in Britain. They represented their flocks politically, partly because they could and partly because nobody else would.* They learned the secrets behind the tenacity of Hebridean Gaelic crofting society. They identified – rightly or wrongly – that cultural tenacity with the stubborn cohesion of Catholic faith in the islands, and they involved themselves as deeply as possible in the everyday work and play of their communities.

They defined themselves in part by what they were not: the Presbyterian ministers who dominated most of the surrounding

---

* The fact that most of them were from the mainland may not have been accidental and probably underpinned their political interventions. 'I think that one of the things which may have influenced the boldness of the priests at that time,' says Father Michael MacDonald, 'was simply that they had no relations on the islands who could have been got at by the estate factor or others.'

Highlands and Islands. Relations were often cordial enough between Highland Catholic priests and Protestant ministers, despite the conviction of one that the other was going to hell and taking his congregation with him. But it became an orthodoxy among Catholics that their denominational rivals were at best dour and joyless and at worst prohibitive of song, story, fun and games. The Catholic priests by contrast presented themselves as inclusive, sociable and tolerant. Father Frederick Odo Blundell would write during the First World War,

> We can learn to appreciate the efforts of our own clergy, whose conduct in this matter differed so greatly from that of many of their Presbyterian contemporaries. Mr Alexander Carmichael, who was far from being a Catholic, but who, as the greatest authority on matters Celtic in recent times, has every claim to our respect, bitterly regrets how the Calvinist ministers did their best by their stern disapproval to stamp out the old Gaelic poetry and customs. He gives instances of how the [Protestant] people of the Isles no longer dare to repeat the old tales to each other ... Mr Carmichael himself was often tantalised by the story or song he had coaxed out of a Highlander being stopped midway by the appearance of the minister or one of the disapproving elders of the district.*

---

* The folklorist Alexander Carmichael's actual words, published in 1900, were: 'Gaelic oral literature has been disappearing during the last three centuries. It is now becoming meagre in quantity, inferior in quality, and greatly isolated. Several causes have contributed towards this decadence – principally the Reformation, the rebellions, the evictions, the Disruption, the schools, and the spirit of the age. Converts in religion, in politics, or in aught else, are apt to be intemperate in speech and rash in action. The Reformation movement condemned the beliefs and cults tolerated and assimilated by the Celtic Church and the Latin Church. Nor did sculpture and architecture escape their intemperate zeal. The rebellions harried and harassed the people, while the evictions impoverished, dispirited, and scattered them over the world. Ignorant school-teaching and clerical narrowness have been painfully detrimental to the expressive language, wholesome literature, manly sports, and interesting amusements of the Highland people.'

Allan MacDonald would tell a story of himself walking down a South Uist road in bad weather, passing a local Protestant elder and happily calling out, 'It's a nasty day, this!'

'It's as the Lord sends,' said the elder.

'Well, it's not his best, then,' said Father Allan, laughing.

The visitor to whom Allan MacDonald told that tale of a wet day in Uist was not completely convinced. She had travelled through Protestant Skye and decided that 'Free-Kirkers have the name of being more strait-laced . . . at two weddings, I found them all merry enough, once the minister was away . . . "They're waiting for me to go before the fun begins", [a Free Church minister] said in my ear at table; a genial man withal, and a well-liked.'

There was certainly a difference on Sundays. The Sabbath was strictly observed, from midnight to midnight, in Presbyterian parishes. When New Year's Day occurred on a Sunday the festivities were solemnly postponed for 24 hours. But as Amy Murray recorded, in the Catholic islands on the seventh day,

> No Gloom, then, Celtic or otherwise, was to be observed . . .
> Ceilidh came at the end of it – the same, but for dancing, as
> on any other night; while before vespers, if it chanced any sort
> of a decent weather, you saw [the] islandry by twos, by tens,
> by twenties, afoot or sitting on the slope before the chapel;
> and the priest, bareheaded and in his soutane, striding round
> amongst them.

If it was a caricature it became self-fulfilling. Catholic priests were alive to the fact that the same word – superstition – was used in the industrial age to disparage Celtic fables and lore and the rituals of their own Church. So one cheerfully embraced the other. Amy Murray wrote that Father Allan MacDonald would have 'No quarrel . . . with the piper nor with the *seanachaidh* [storyteller, tradition-bearer], nor even with whisky in moderation. "We know how necessary it is for our poor people to be happy", I have heard him say.'

They were also young men who had travelled widely and studied deeply. They had what would become known as personal hinterlands. In Bornish, Daliburgh and Barra, where there were no lending libraries, no scientific and literary associations, very few newspapers and only occasional mail, those hinterlands assumed great importance. Some of the young priests hunted and fished. Some of them played chess and cards. Some of them played football and shinty. Some of them wrote poetry. Some of them studied the Gaelic language and its deep well of surviving folklore and song. 'It would be satisfactory to know,' wrote Father Allan MacDonald later of two young students for the priesthood, 'that each of them had a liking for some byestudy. Such a study is a lifelong joy and recreation, and needed where one is isolated.'

In the early 1880s there were 3,800 people in South Uist. Most of them, some 2,300, spoke only Gaelic. Another 1,300 spoke Gaelic and varying amounts of English. Only 173 human beings in the whole population were not Gaelic speakers. They were chiefly inarticulate, newly born babies. The rest were members of what John Lorne Campbell called the 'very small middle class . . . [the estate] factor on the island and his subordinates . . . about half a dozen big farmers holding leases from the estate; and the doctor, a few merchants, hotel-keepers, schoolmasters and government officials'. Some of that small middle class did speak Gaelic but some did not. The other 3,600 people when Father Allan MacDonald arrived in South Uist in July 1884 were either landless cottars scratching a living on the shore or crofting 'tenants-at-will': crofters and their families without security of tenure of their cottages, patches of arable land, peat cuttings and grazing moor. One eviction notice could turn, overnight, a working crofter and his family into landless and homeless cottars. The painful results of that feudalism had, in 1883, sent Lord Napier and his commissioners to discover the condition and determine the future of the crofters and cottars of northern Scotland.

Without feasible exception, every member of South Uist's

3,600-strong crofting community was a Gaelic speaker. Most of them, all but a few hundred, were also traditional Roman Catholics. Allan MacDonald had finally arrived among the last living remnants of the Celtic Church.

In the second half of the nineteenth century the entire chain of Catholic islands in the Outer Hebrides, from Barra Head to Benbecula, was owned by one family. They had been bought in 1838 from their bankrupt hereditary clan chiefs by a 55-year-old Aberdeenshire landowner named John Gordon. Early in the nineteenth century Colonel John Gordon had pursued a 20-year career in the Aberdeenshire Militia. He travelled extensively, especially in Egypt, where he carved his name on at least 14 Pharaonic tombs and temples, and he became Member of Parliament for Weymouth and Melcombe Regis on the south coast of England. Following his father's death in 1814 Gordon inherited the family's substantial estates in the West Indies and north-eastern Scotland. He became a property speculator before the term was coined. From his baronial base at the Castle of Cluny, 15 miles inland from Aberdeen, John Gordon proceeded to acquire further swathes of rural Aberdeenshire as well as the southern Outer Hebrides. By the 1840s John Gordon was judged to be the richest commoner in Scotland. He was 'above the middle-size, of stout athletic build and possessed a hardy constitution'. He was also, as the people of South Uist would discover, a martinet, a Georgian country squire whose eighteenth-century heritage and military background informed his attitude towards his civilian tenantry.

Colonel John Gordon never married but he fathered several children (some of whom he recognised and adopted) by different women. The oldest of his acknowledged male offspring was 'born in fornication', as the parish register recorded, to a woman named Margaret MacKay at the end of December 1820 in the Nairnshire village of Auldearn. The boy was named for his father, John Gordon, and taken to be raised at Cluny Castle. There John Gordon junior lived the genteel life of a single heir. He married when young but was quickly widowed. He returned to his leisurely bachelor life: perusing the family's estates; travelling between the city lights and the country acres; granting his services as an Aberdeenshire Justice of the Peace. Upon his father's death at their Edinburgh townhouse in 1858, John Gordon inherited upwards of £2,000,000,* as well as large portions of Scotland, including the island of South Uist.

On inheriting his estate at the age of 37 John Gordon became one of the most eligible widowers in Britain. When he was 44 he married again. His new wife was 20 years old and an orphan. Emily Eliza Steele Pringle was a child of Empire: she had been born in Madras to an officer of the Indian Civil Service. Although she would display little future interest in the country, Emily Pringle brimmed with the blue blood of Scotland. Her paternal grandfather was Sir John Pringle of Stichill in Roxburghshire, and her grandmother was a daughter of the 23rd MacLeod of MacLeod. Her mother, Hester Helen McNeill, was the daughter of General Malcolm McNeill, who served with distinction in the Indian Army. When General McNeill was based in Madras his daughter Hester met there the local civil servant John Robert Pringle. They married in 1844. Emily was born in the following year. In 1847, when she was two years old, her father died. Her mother soon followed him. Emily Pringle returned, parentless, to the Scottish borders and the care of relatives.

John Gordon and Emily Pringle were married at St John's Episcopal Church in Edinburgh shortly before Christmas in 1865, and promptly set up house with a dozen servants in London's Park Lane. What the people of South Uist and its surrounding islands would come to know as the long, distant reign of Lady Gordon Cathcart was about to begin.

---

* Insofar as it is possible to calculate such things, the capital value of £2,000,000 in 1858 would have been worth at least £150,000,000 in 2010. Its comparative purchasing power was closer to ten times that amount. Margaret MacKay's son was a billionaire.

By 1858, when John Gordon inherited the Catholic Hebrides from his father, most of the damage had already been done by his family to those islands. The middle-aged millionaire could afford to be magnanimous to his Gaelic tenantry. John Gordon junior was not his father's boy. He was shy and diffident where Colonel John had been active, autocratic and ruthless. He seemed genuinely impressed by the men and women of the islands. 'The Uist people are born gentlemen – Nature's noblemen,' this illegitimate son of a Nairnshire village girl was reported as telling an acquaintance. It was in no degree an opinion which could have issued from his father.

But in 1878, while Allan MacDonald was studying at Valladolid, John Gordon died. He was 57 years old. His widow was 33. As their union had been childless Emily Gordon was specifically conveyed the family's Hebridean estate by her late husband's will. Two years later, in 1880, she married a baronet in London. The 40-year-old Sir Reginald Cathcart was a scion of the lesser Gloucestershire peerage. His new wife became Lady Emily Cathcart. They set up home in the exclusive demesne of Sunninghill within the Royal Borough of Windsor and Maidenhead in Berkshire.

Reginald Archibald Edward Cathcart enjoyed his new wife's Hebridean shooting and fishing estate. He would retire irregularly to South Uist, taking up residence at Grogarry House in the north of the island, attended to there by half a dozen imported servants and 15 or 16 islanders employed for the occasion. 'Sometimes he would come for grouse-shooting or trout-fishing,' the schoolteacher Frederick Rea would report, 'but only stayed a month or so at a time. Several times he came with some servants to the inn at Polachar and went out seal-shooting with the landlord . . .' Sir Reginald had sufficient regard for his northern resort to repair and extend Grogarry House, and commission 'a professional golfer from St Andrews' to design an 18-hole course on the west coast machair at Askernish.

Apart from the hired help, he usually travelled alone. It would later be suggested that in the entirety of her 67-year stewardship of the island, between her marriage to John Gordon in 1865 and her death in 1932, Lady Emily Gordon Cathcart visited South Uist only once. If so, Frederick Rea caught a glimpse of her on that occasion. The teacher and a friend were driving north in a pony-and-trap along the single arterial road. After a few miles

> ... we slackened pace at seeing ahead a large phaeton drawn up on the grass verging the road.
>
> As we passed by I judged that the equipage must belong to an important personage: a liveried coachman and footman with cockaded hats stood by the heads of the two well-groomed horses, whose highly-polished harness glistened in the sunshine. On the grass near the vehicle several dead grouse lay. At a bend of the road a little further on a lady was approaching, and I noticed, as we passed her, that she was of tall, handsome and commanding appearance, and was carrying a small dog in her arms.
>
> She bowed as we raised our caps in passing, and immediately afterwards as we drove on Alasdair said: 'Lady Cathcart ...!'

Emily Pringle had come a long way from Madras.

Visitors and residents alike often experienced the Gordon Cathcart Estate's South Uist as a bleak and unpromising place. Her courteous bow to Frederick Rea notwithstanding, Lady Gordon Cathcart was an imperious aristocrat, a committed combatant in the class war who opposed at every turn her tenants' struggles for security. Through her estate agent she argued vigorously against any reform of the landholding system.

She operated pettily and vindictively. In 1888 she felt obliged to sue 34 Uist and Barra crofters who had fallen behind in rental payments to an average amount of £50 each. Instead of raising the cases in Lochmaddy Sheriff Court in North Uist, which the defendants could comfortably have attended and where they could have presented their defences or mitigations, Lady Gordon

Cathcart deliberately took out the summonses at the Court of Session in Edinburgh – 'hundreds of miles from their homes', as the Inverness-shire MP Charles Fraser-Mackintosh said – to which no Uist crofter, let alone one whose rent was in arrears, could afford to travel. Add to that distance the fact that Edinburgh was a city in which few Uist crofters of the 1880s would have been able to make themselves understood on the street, let alone argue a legal case, and the proprietrix's action seemed to be motivated more by malice than a principled desire to uphold the law.

She may also have intended to inflict more than discomfort. Father Allan MacDonald noted in his journal ten years later

> How simple it would be for a proprietor in these parts to get all the people here out of the benefits of the Crofters' Act [which had passed two years before Lady Gordon Cathcart's lawsuit against the 34 crofters] by conniving with a merchant to get them hopelessly in debt, and then have them declared bankrupt by which their rights as crofters would be forfeited.

When in 1890 the telegraph facility at the post office in the well-populated township of Howmore was closed, she paid the Postmaster General to reopen it – but three miles away in Grogarry, where almost nobody lived but Lady Emily and Sir Reginald Cathcart during their infrequent visits.

Later that same year Charles Fraser-Mackintosh MP raised the issue of Lady Gordon Cathcart's behaviour in the House of Commons.

> I beg to ask the Lord Advocate, whether he is aware that the large island of South Uist is divided the one half and richer among 12 farmers, and the other and poorer among 1,250 families; that the Crofters have been in use to gather for sale the perishable commodity of sea ware called tangles, not only on the shores of their own lands, but also on those of the large farmers, without let or hindrance; but that, so soon as the

Crofters, who had formerly considered themselves bound to sell to the proprietrix, understood they were entitled to free market, and began their operations this season in usual form, the proprietrix instigated some of the larger tenants, who do not themselves engage in the work, to interdict the Crofters from pursuing their occupation, and has in her own and their name instituted process to this effect in the highest and most expensive legal Court in Scotland; whether he is aware that, at a great open-air meeting held at Daliburgh on 16 June, the people loudly complained of their treatment, and demanded legislative redress; and whether he will take steps to legislate for the relief of the people primarily interested, and against the closing of a valuable chemical trade?

The Lord Advocate declined to intervene.

When she made landfall in 1894, Father Allan MacDonald's acquaintance Ada Goodrich-Freer thought the island to be the epitome of 'poverty, misery, neglect ... South Uist is surely the most forsaken spot on God's earth'.

Its condition, she considered, was owed to those 12 tenant farms which sprawled across the western coastal plain –

> ... a 'farm' here signifying a tract of country once bright with happy homesteads, now laid bare and desolate. Heaps of grey stone scattered all over the island are all that remain of hundreds of once thriving cottages; narrow strips of greener grass or more tender heather are all that is left to represent waving cornfields and plots of fertile ground handed on from generation to generation of home-loving agriculturalists.
>
> The more hardy and vigorous of the race which once flourished here are now scattered over the face of the earth; the old, the weak, the spiritless, for the most part, have alone remained, and their children, white-faced, anaemic, depressed, driven to the edge of the sea as one after another the scraps of land redeemed by their perilous industry were taken from

them, are still fighting hand-to-hand with Nature, almost worn out with a hopeless struggle. They are the only Highlanders I ever met who were curt in manner, almost inhospitable, discourteous . . .

Ada Goodrich-Freer was not a thorough or a balanced reporter. Her impressions of a brief visit to South Uist were untypical and unreliable. But she managed to echo, however hysterically, a half-digested version of the recent history of South Uist as it was conveyed to her by Father Allan and his fellow priests. South Uist might never have been a perfect idyll 'bright with happy homesteads'. But it had, just a short time earlier, been a place of relative stability.

In 1841 the population of South Uist was 5,093. In 1861, after 23 years under Colonel John Gordon of Cluny Castle, it had been reduced to 3,406. During two decades in which the population of the rest of Scotland increased by 17 per cent, from 2,620,184 to 3,062,294, the population of the island of South Uist fell by 33 per cent.

It did not happen accidentally. 'We have suffered many injustices,' a 75-year-old crofter from Kilphedar named John MacKay told the Napier Commission in Lochboisdale in May 1883:

We were not allowed to keep a dog, though we would pay licence for it. Our sheep were chased and gathered to a certain place called a fank by the [estate's] ground officer, constables, and other helpers, through the order of the factor, in order to see if any crofter had more than ten sheep, which was the number allowed for us to keep however high the rent of the croft might be . . . we were deprived of our former hill pasturage, which we claim and trust to get possession of yet. Ground officer and constables used to come two or three days before the market's day to our houses, marking our stock which was ready for the market, compelling us to drive them to the factor's house, so as to avoid us the freedom of selling them at the market ourselves. We were obliged to make potato parks to the proprietrix on our rented land; which we cultivated from mere wild moor with crooked and common spades... Our peats stance has been taken from us to make room for crofters and cottars, where they have a miserable living...

If we complain of being overcrowded, the factor's answer is, 'There is no room for the people in the country.' Yes, there is plenty for twice or thrice as many, from where others were driven and compelled to emigrate to America; some of whom had been tied before our eyes, others hiding themselves in caves and crevices for fear of being caught by authorised officers.

A member of the commission wondered aloud if life in South Uist really had been better when John MacKay was a younger man, before the tenant farms were staked out and fenced off, before the clearances and emigrations of the middle of the nineteenth century.

'We were very much better off in food and clothing when I was young,' said the 75-year-old. 'When I was a young man, I would complain very much of the food I take today... We had butter, cheese, flesh, potatoes, and meal, of which we cannot today partake, and plenty of them, of which today there is very little.'

John MacKay was asked shortly afterwards to substantiate his claims of forced emigration in 1850 and 1851, and of the complicity of police officers in estate clearance policy. He said:

I saw a policeman chasing a man down the macher towards Askernish, with a view to catch him, in order to send him on board an emigrant ship lying in Loch Boisdale. I saw a man who lay down on his face and nose on a little island, hiding himself from the policeman, and the policeman getting a dog to search for this missing man in order to get him on board the emigrant ship... A man named Angus Johnston, whose wife gave birth to three children... he was seized and tied upon the pier of Loch Boisdale; and it was by means of giving him a kick that he was put into the boat and knocked down. The old

priest interfered, and said, 'What are you doing to this man?
Let him alone. It is against the law ...'

The estate of Colonel John Gordon and its supporters said that
such tales were lurid fantasies. That provoked an angry written
response from Father Donald Mackintosh, who had been a priest
in South Uist between 1861 and 1877. When he arrived in the
island ten years afterwards, said Father Mackintosh, 'the clearances
in 1851, and the emigration, forced in some circumstances with
shocking inhumanity, were fresh in the memory of old and
young... They [the Uist crofters] did not exaggerate. Indeed,
in describing things that happened in those times, to exaggerate
would not be easy.'

Their suspicion that there had been a sectarian impulse behind
some of the Highland Clearances informed the liberation theology of those Hebridean priests. They knew that Protestant
Highlanders had also suffered eviction and forced emigration. But
they wondered if Roman Catholics had been disproportionately
cleared. The previous 300 years gave them cause to suppose that
their co-religionists had on some occasions been victimised by
Protestant estate owners and their employees.

It was a difficult opinion to sustain and an easy one to scorn.
Over the whole of the nineteenth century, many more Protestants
than Catholics were cleared or had emigrated from the Highlands
and Islands. Although there were many more Protestants than
Catholics to clear in the first place, the dispossession of thousands
of Protestants from Sutherland, Ross-shire, Skye and elsewhere
argued that the evictions were non-denominational. There is
also evidence, after the Disruption of the Church of Scotland
in 1843, of seceding Free Church men who were involved in, or
even merely supportive of, the Highland land struggle being
singled out for special abuse by the agents of Established Church
or Episcopalian landowners. Many Protestant ministers spoke
out against Clearances, and many Protestant landowners refused

to clear. Conversely, the ruthless, clearing landlord Alasdair Ranaldson MacDonell of Glengarry came from an old Catholic family, which did not stay his hand from evicting his own superfluous Catholic tenants-at-will.

In their purest form the Clearances of counties like Sutherland and islands like South Uist were the result of a secular economic philosophy. The eighteenth- and nineteenth-century 'improvers' who argued that the thin soil of the Highlands and Islands would be more profitable if it were turned over to large tenant farms or sheep ranches, were quite unconcerned about the religious faith of the settled inhabitants who would have to be moved.

In one sense, however, the intuition of the Catholic priests was correct. 'Improvement' policies were a product of the Scottish Enlightenment. They elevated reason above sentiment, and intellectual and fiscal discipline above feudal indulgence. The doctrine of improvement was ecumenical, but it rejected the old world and sought a logical new order in human affairs. That was vastly easier for a Reformed Protestant than an unreconstructed Roman Catholic to accept. Patrick Sellar, the pioneering clearing agent of the Sutherland estate, was a Presbyterian Scot who rejoiced in the triumph of 'sense and goodness' over 'bigotry and superstition' – 'bigotry and superstition' being in early nineteenth-century Scotland synonyms for 'Roman Catholicism'. The sceptical free-market economist Adam Smith could not have been a Roman Catholic. Fathers Donald Mackintosh, James Chisholm and Allan MacDonald could never have been 'improvers'.

Those priests were not naturally sectarian. On a practical social level, they could not afford to be. Friendships with their parishioners were judged unsuitable, and to avoid an eremitic existence many of them, including Father Allan MacDonald, socialised with Protestant members of the local merchant and professional classes. But they were not absorbed by the harsh Clearances of Protestant islands and parishes elsewhere in the north of Scotland. Their sympathies were monopolised by the persecution of their small, precious Catholic communities in Knoydart, Canna and South Uist. Having survived two centuries of what certainly had been sectarian discrimination, for those congregations to find themselves on the front line of another 100 years of economic warfare seemed just too much to bear.

Such circumstances generated a reaction not only from the priests and some radical politicians, but also from the people themselves. In 1886 the House of Commons was informed of 'a printed statement, lately issued by the proprietrix of South Uist [Lady Emily Gordon Cathcart], where it is alleged that outrages were committed by paraffin being put in her [Established] church pew, by telegraph lines being cut, and the terrorism prevailing was such that the perpetrators of these crimes could not be discovered by the authorities, although well known in the district . . .'

Island priests, who could hardly approve of churches of any denomination being vandalised, had frequently to walk a narrow line between supporting their parishioners' rights and discouraging them from excess. But whether it was for denominational or political reasons, there was frequent bad feeling between priests and the landowning establishment in South Uist. In the middle of the nineteenth century Father John Chisholm of Bornish involved himself in regular skirmishes with the estate factor of the time, one of which famously caused the factor to shake his fist in the priest's face at a public meeting. Allan MacDonald's friend Father John Mackintosh was,

> . . . in a constant war with the farmer at Bornish, Donald Ferguson, who was hated by the people. There is a story that Ferguson and his associates partly severed the traces to Father John's gig while he was in Lochboisdale one day, and tied tin cans to the back of the gig. The idea was that the cans woud 'spook' the horse and the tension put on the traces would mean that the gig would crash. A Protestant shopkeeper in Lochboisdale alerted the priest and saved the day!

It is possible that similar unpleasantnesses created the vacancy in Daliburgh which was filled by Father Allan MacDonald.

Following his own public presentation to the Napier Commission of the case for Catholic schoolteachers in South Uist, the 29-year-old incumbent at Daliburgh, Father Sandy Mackintosh, was, in his own words, 'regarded by some as endeavouring to stir up feelings of religious animosity among our people'. It was a charge which he emphatically denied. But it was clearly troublesome to the young priest, not least because the 'some' who had chosen to regard him in this unfavourable light were people of influence and power. Father Mackintosh was a first cousin of Allan MacDonald: their mothers had been sisters. He had been at Daliburgh for only two years, since 1881, but the politics of the situation may have caused his transfer from the island to Fort William shortly afterwards – and paved the way for his replacement in South Uist in 1884 by his cousin.

Father Allan arrived in South Uist in the summer. 'On Saturday, 19th July, 1884,' wrote John Lorne Campbell, 'a tall, energetic, ascetic young Highland priest, Fr Allan McDonald, landed at Lochboisdale in the island of South Uist in the Outer Hebrides to take charge of the parish of Daliburgh, or Dalibrog . . .'

The days were long and warm. The slopes of the rocky hills on the east side of the long island were dark green in the morning sun. The rolling, fertile machair land of the western seaboard was alive with primroses, clover and violets, marigolds, gentians and orchids, eyebright, buttercups and daisies. Peats cut out of the bog a few months earlier were still drying on the rough turf. Lapwings, dunlins, buntings, whooper swans, redshanks and a dozen other avian species fluttered and glided overhead. In the long afternoons opalescent light reflected milkily off the inland lochs. Beyond the houses on the machair the blue Atlantic Ocean foamed and broke on a ribbon of clean white sand that ran for 20 miles along the western shore. In such seasons South Uist was very far from being the most forsaken spot on God's earth.

He settled carefully into his first parish. He moved into the priest's house by St Peter's Church at the edge of Daliburgh machair, between the head of Loch Boisdale and the west coast dunes. St Peter's had been built with 500 sittings just 16 years earlier to serve the biggest parish in South Uist. In the 1860s a small chapel stood on its consecrated ground. When the large edifice of St Peter's was raised in 1868 by Father Alexander Campbell of Bornish and his junior priest Donald McColl, 'the old [chapel] was allowed to stand, the new walls were built round it, and the roof placed over them, after which the old building was removed from within the new'.

Daliburgh was the southernmost as well as the largest of the three Roman Catholic parishes in South Uist. Its 1,600 parishioners lived in the west coast machair crofting townships which trailed from Askernish through Daliburgh, Kilphedar, Boisdale, Garrynamonie and Smerclete. Just beyond Smerclete, at Polachar on the south-western tip of the island, an inn stood looking over the wide sound to Barra. The small fishing and crofting communities of Kilbride and Ludag straggled along the rocky south coast towards the island of Eriskay, whose 460 people sat a mile offshore but were nonetheless part of Daliburgh parish and part of the School Board District of South Uist. More houses ran through South and North Glendale, and into the waterside hamlet of South Lochboisdale. Halfway down the deep sea entrance of Loch Boisdale – 'one of the safest and most capacious harbours in the Hebrides; and offers a favourite retreat to storm-tossed passing vessels' according to a reporter in the early 1880s – the steamers from Glasgow and Oban docked beside a fine hotel and a telegraph office.

Nobody lived on the eastern hills and very few people lived on the eastern shore. The *Gazetteer* of 1884 explained,

The soil on the uplands is so barren as mostly to afford but poor pasturage; on the tracts between the uplands and the lakes is partly black loam and partly moss; on the western seaboard, from end to end of that tract, over a breadth varying between ½ mile and 1 mile, is all sand; on the most productive arable grounds is an artificial mixture of sand, black earth, and manure. The uplands are devoted chiefly to the rearing of black cattle, to the improvement of which by the introduction of new breeds, great attention has for some time been paid. The middle tract or belt of low country along the W[estern] base of the uplands is partly firm ground, naturally drained by runnels into the lake, and under cultivation, and partly black peaty moss undergoing gradual amelioration from diffusion on it of drift calcareous sand. The low sandy belt along the W[estern] shore is all arable, and produces, with aid of ordinary manures, good crops of oats, barley, and potatoes. Agriculture as a rule is conducted on thriftless principles . . .

Those were the men, women and children of Father Allan's first congregation: hardy and independent souls whose preferred lifestyle involved growing grain and root vegetables on the 'low, flat and sandy' western plain, summer grazing their cattle and sheep on the infertile uplands, catching fish from the sea to sell and poaching fish from the estate's inland lochs to eat, cutting their year's fuel from the 'black peaty moss' of the 'middle belt' of their island, and living in their low, stone, thatched houses.

Alexander Carmichael, who knew them well, wrote:

The people of the Outer Isles, like the people of the Highlands and Islands generally, are simple and law-abiding, common crime being rare and serious crime unknown among them. They are good to the poor, kind to the stranger, and courteous to all. During all the years that I lived and travelled among them [throughout the second half of the nineteenth century], night and day, I never met with incivility, never with rudeness, never with vulgarity, never with aught but courtesy. I never entered a house without the inmates offering me food or apologising for their want of it. I never was asked for charity in the West, a striking contrast to my experience in England, where I was frequently asked for food, for drink, for money, and that by persons whose incomes would have been wealth to the poor men and women of the West.

As Carmichael had discovered to his delight, the Uibhistich (people of Uist) still held, in the 1880s, to many of their old religious and secular Celtic traditions. The Fort Augustus monk and Church historian Frederick Odo Blundell would write 30 years later:

At Christmas three Masses were said, one immediately after the other, at midnight. Most of the men would bring their shinty clubs even to the midnight Mass, and at dawn would go not home but to the Machar for shinty. Even the old men would put off their shoes for the game, and there would be a small mountain of shoes at the goal. For the Christmas dinner, each household invariably killed a sheep, and had the best repast of the year.

On New Year's Eve boys and young men would go from house to house and would have to say their piece of poetry before the door would be opened. Then they would go round the fire by the left. The fire, be it noted, was always in the centre of the floor in those days and before they sat down would say: 'God bless the house and all its contents.' To which [the priest] or the oldest person present would say: 'God bless you! God bless you!' This custom is still kept up.

For Purification, candles were made of tallow and peat ashes, needless to say between folds of linen, and these candles were coloured blue, red, etc., to make them look festive. I brought back from Uist one of these candles and lit it at a meeting of the Society of Antiquaries at Inverness, when everyone was surprised to see how well it burned.

At Easter the children would go from house to house gathering eggs, and would then play amongst themselves. One would strike his egg against that of his opponent, and the winner would have whichever cracked. People would rise early on Easter morning to see the sun rise, believing that it danced for joy.

St Michael's Day, or Michaelmas, was a great feast, and was kept as a Holiday of Obligation. Sports were held on the Machar, especially horse races, which took place at Ardmichel, a tongue of land midway between Bornish and Howbeg, and exactly half-way between the north and south ends of the island. In the evening there was a ball in every township. At Michaelmas also a special cake was made, one for each member of the family, and others would be sent as a remembrance to friends in Glasgow and elsewhere.

St Andrew's Day was the beginning of the shinty season, which afforded endless amusement during the winter afternoons, whilst the evenings were enlivened with song and story, the bagpipe and the fiddle, several of which may still be seen in almost every cottage. Little wonder that Catholic Uist should have been a happy home where the ancient ballads survived better than elsewhere.

In the late nineteenth century Alexander Carmichael wrote,

There is a tradition among the people of the Western Isles that Christ required Peter to row 707 strokes straight out from the shore when He commanded him to go and procure the fish containing the tribute-money. Following this tradition, the old men of Uist require the young men to row 707 strokes from the land before casting their lines on Christmas Day. And whatever fish they get are cordially given to the needy as a tribute in the name of Christ, King of the sea, and of Peter, king of fishermen. This is called 'dioladh deirc', tribute-paying, 'deirce Pheadair', Peter's tribute, 'dioladh Pheadail', Peter's payment, and other terms. This tribute-paying on Christmas Day excites much emotional interest, and all try to enhance the tribute and in various ways to render the alms as substantial as possible.

After he had told the Napier Commission at Lochboisdale in 1883 of the 'many injustices' suffered by his people, the 75-year-old Kilphedar crofter John MacKay was asked by a commissioner from Skye: 'But they have not given up singing songs, I hope?'

'Oh no,' said John MacKay, 'they have not given up songs.'

'And they have not given up piping?'

'No.'

South Uist was known and admired throughout the Scottish Gaidhealtachd and beyond for its music, fable, verse and song. As we have seen, most Roman Catholics were in little doubt that the depth of this living oral and instrumental tradition was bound to the resilience of Uist Catholicism. Protestant ministers, they were keen to argue, had since the Reformation tried 'by their stern disapproval to stamp out the old Gaelic poetry and customs'. Whether the strength of such traditions in South Uist was owed to a benign priesthood or to the island's proud and self-sufficient isolation – whether or not Catholicism itself had survived in Uist for the same unique geographical and historical reasons that had preserved the Gaelic language and its affiliated music and legend – nobody could dispute their miraculous existence. South Uist was and would remain a treasure-trove for Celtic folklorists.

If Allan MacDonald needed a guide to the island's inner depths, he found one instantly. When Allan's friend John Mackintosh moved in 1883 to Bornish, the parish to the north of Daliburgh in South Uist, Father John replaced the 65-year-old resident priest Alexander Campbell. Father Campbell, a native of South Uist, then moved down to the priest's house by the church of St Peter's at Daliburgh which he had been instrumental in building 15 years earlier. He was living there – registered as a retired Roman Catholic clergyman – when Allan MacDonald arrived in 1884, and the old man would stay there until his death nine years later.

It was certainly the intention of Bishop Angus MacDonald to put the fledgling Allan MacDonald under the wing of Alexander

Campbell, and it worked. The two men made good housemates. Father Alexander had been born and raised in South Uist before Queen Victoria climbed onto the throne. Alexander Campbell told Allan MacDonald that 'There are two kinds of priests that don't get on well with the Islesmen. Those who make themselves too friendly, and those who don't make themselves friendly enough.' He helped to polish the remaining imperfections in Father Allan's conversational Gaelic. He would have instructed his young protégé in Uist devotional customs: those three Christmas night Masses; the New Year's Eve and Easter rituals; the Michaelmas Holy Day events; the Purification candles. He watched paternally as the young priest found his footing. 'For the first few Sundays after I came to Dalibrog,' said Father Allan, 'I went along quietly enough. Then all at once I put a great smoke out of myself in the pulpit; and when the people were going home they were saying to each other, "There's something *in* the long fair man!"'

Alexander Campbell was also a good escort to the folklore of the island. In 1871, when he was still at Bornish, Father Alexander had assisted the great collector Alexander Carmichael on one of Carmichael's many field trips to the island. 'My boy,' the elderly Father Alexander told the young Father Allan, 'when you've ploughed what I've harrowed, you'll believe more things.' By his mid-twenties Allan MacDonald did not need anybody to inspire his love of the Gaelic language, and he might not have required a fellow enthusiast to interest him in Gaelic lore. But the regular company of an elderly fellow priest who had been brought up speaking no other language and was immersed in its associated Celtic culture concentrated his mind. From that point onwards there would be little doubt about Allan MacDonald's preferred private hinterland, or 'byestudy'. It lay all around him in the language, culture and history of the Catholic Outer Hebrides.

In the short term he had political work to do. The Napier Commission had acknowledged in its final report in 1884 the Protestant-dominated School Board and teacher controversy in the Catholic Hebrides. Napier wrote:

It has ... been represented to us as a grievance ... that under the present administration of the [1872 Education] Act in South Uist and Barra, where the majority of the population are Roman Catholics, due regard has not been shown, in the selection of teachers, to the religious principles of the majority of the population.

If this contention is well-founded, and if the School Board, as at present constituted, should not hereafter give due consideration to the wishes of their constituents, the remedy is in the hands of the ratepayers at any ensuing election of the Boards.

The Napier Commission's faith in the democratic process was undiminished by the warning of Father James Chisholm that in South Uist and Barra Catholic crofting ratepayers 'were deterred by fear [of eviction] from exercising that right'. Or perhaps Lord Napier and his commissioners were aware that their report from the Highlands and Islands might provoke legislation which would remove the fear of eviction from crofting households.

The next elections to South Uist School Board were scheduled to take place in the spring of 1888. Two years before that, in June 1886, the Liberal Party majority in the United Kingdom parliament responded to the Napier Report by passing a Crofters' Act. The Crofters' Holdings (Scotland) Act of 1886 would be described as 'the Magna Carta of the Highlands and Islands'. It legislated for fair rents, compensation for improvements to land and property, and above all security of tenure to crofters in South Uist, Barra and everywhere else in the north and west of Scotland. The days of the crofting tenant-at-will were over. There would be – there could be – no more mass Clearances from the Highlands. The men of that large region, whatever their language or religion, could after 1886 exercise their right to vote in local and national elections without the threat of serious reprisal.

A year earlier, at the end of 1885, the first General Election following the Third Reform Act had taken place. The Third

Reform Act enfranchised most crofters for the first time. The result in the Highlands and Islands was little short of revolutionary. Previously the few privileged voters in crofting counties such as Inverness-shire, which contained South Uist, had returned – often without even the charade of a contest – titled grandees to parliament. In 1885, when the crofters' vote was counted, they rejected all of the noble landowners and in a series of landslides elected radical 'crofters' candidates' to represent them.

There was therefore a manifold emancipation at work among the crofters of Uist and Barra. After 1832 the more affluent members of their Roman Catholic faith were, for the first time in modern history, permitted to vote. Fifty years later most ordinary crofters, whatever their religion, were also enfranchised. In the 1885 General Election they demonstrated, not least to themselves, the startling power of the free ballot. In 1886 the Crofters' Act removed their remaining fears of victimisation if they voted against the landowning interest. The stage was perfectly set for an upheaval in the School Board elections of 1888.

Father Allan MacDonald campaigned for a majority Catholic representation on the South Uist School Board in the spring of 1888. That is established by the fact that he himself, the 28-year-old priest from Fort William, stood for election to the Board. It is, however, probable that in 1888 Father Allan was following his bishop's rather than his own inclinations. A private and slightly introverted young man, Allan MacDonald would later confess, 'How little I liked to be drawn into serious conversation about these [local political] things. They so annoy and worry me – the discussion of the disagreeableness attached to these duties.' But he understood the corrosive effect of a landowning autocracy on the character of its tenants – the imposition of a 'disheartening Estate management, which takes the soul out of a poor man and degrades his character' – and of the urgent need to improve the condition and morale of his congregation.

The fact that a Catholic majority on the seven-strong School Board following free elections was the settled will of the South Uist people was proved by the result. The old Protestant majority of five to two was overthrown and replaced by a representation of four Catholics and three Protestants. The case for a Catholic majority would not have been a difficult argument to win with most of the voting men of South Uist. Apart from its contemporary merits, the debate stirred folk memories of a century earlier. In the 1760s a hereditary South Uist landowner, Alasdair Mor MacDonald of Boisdale, converted from Catholicism to Protestantism. According to a memorial published by the Catholic Church shortly afterwards, MacDonald of Boisdale then

> ... took the resolution to cause all the people under him to embrace the Protestant religion and to extinguish the old religion entirely as far as his power reached.
>
> To do this his first step was to invite all the children in the neighbourhood to learn English and writing with a Presbyterian preceptor whom he engaged in his family for the education of his own children. This the poor people, suspecting no harm, gladly agreed to, and numbers of children were sent accordingly; but how greatly were their parents astonished, when after some time they understood that ... impious blasphemies had been daily inculcated into them against their religion; that wicked, immoral and even immodest sentences had been given to be copied over by those who could write, and that when the time of Lent came, in the year 1770, flesh meat was forced into the mouths of those who refused to eat it, in contempt of the laws and practice of the Church in that holy season.
>
> No sooner were the parents apprised of these things, than with one accord they called their children home, and absolutely refused to allow them to frequent such a school any longer ...

With such legend in the air, the South Uist School Board election results of 1888 were remarkable more for returning three Protestants than for electing four Catholics. Given a free hand,

South Uist voters were not so dogmatic or vindictive as might have been feared. 'The manner and bearing of the people,' Allan MacDonald wrote to Bishop Angus MacDonald in Oban after the election, 'was most consoling to one who has been even only a few years here. They spoke out manfully and defiantly – a great contrast to the last election.'

Father Allan MacDonald was one of the four Catholics elected. It was his first and his last adventure in electoral politics. But it was a successful excursion. He was immediately elected chairman of the board by his colleagues, and he quickly achieved Bishop Angus MacDonald's 'redress for the people'. In 1889 the Protestant headmistress retired from her post at the school at Garrynamonie, south of Daliburgh, which taught 140 boys and girls from the west coast machair townships in Father Allan's parish. The new chairman and his majority on South Uist School Board asserted themselves by advertising the post in the national Catholic press.

Their advertisement was answered by an adventurous 21-year-old qualified teacher from Worcestershire in the English midlands called Frederick George Rea. Frederick Rea was a practising Roman Catholic. 'According to his testimonials,' Allan MacDonald told Bishop Angus, 'he is an excellent Christian and an able Teacher.' In the last days of December 1889 Frederick Rea packed his belongings and left England on the long train and ferry journey to South Uist. He would begin his new job as head teacher at Garrynamonie when school recommenced after New Year, on 2 January 1890.

He boarded the steamer out of Oban long before dawn on Monday, 30 December, and disembarked in the Hebrides in the middle of the same afternoon. Father Allan was waiting to meet him on Lochboisdale jetty. Rea would recall,

A few men were grouped on the little pier, among whom stood a tall figure clad in clerical black. As I reached the end of the gangway on to the pier, this figure left the group and advanced towards me with extended hand. 'You are the new schoolmaster, I believe,' he said in a deep, strong voice, and with a stronger grasp of the hand. He was a well-proportioned figure, over six feet in height with strongly marked weather-beaten features, about thirty years of age,* and his grey eyes under bushy sandy-coloured eyebrows bent upon me kindly but penetrating looks.

Father Allan seized Frederick Rea's bag and the two men set off 'through driving misty rain along a rough stony road' to walk the three miles from Lochboisdale to the priest's house in Daliburgh. They approached the lights of the house as darkness fell, went through the stone gateway, hung up their wet clothes in a small passage lit by a paraffin lamp and sat down by a peat fire in,

> . . . a small, poorly but comfortably furnished sitting-room . . .
>
> After we had warmed ourselves at the fire a frugal meal was laid on the table by an oldish woman with a weather-beaten but kindly face. My host became more conversational, under the influence of food and warmth. Almost the first thing he said during the meal, as he looked across the table, was: 'I am glad!'
>
> On my asking of what he was glad, he exclaimed: 'Your English is so clear, and anyone can easily understand every word you say.'

Having brought a non-Gaelic-speaking head teacher from the English midlands to South Uist, Father Allan had been understandably concerned that Frederick Rea's dialect would be incomprehensible.

As a large part of his job was to educate children in and then through the English language, Frederick Rea's ignorance of Gaelic was not considered to be an obstacle. Rea was assisted

---

* Father Allan was indeed then 30 years old and 6' 3" tall. The last statistic would cause the people of South Uist, who generally stood several inches shorter, to dub him 'the High Priest'.

at Garrynamonie by pupil–teachers who were native Gaelic speakers. One woman who entered his school 'at the early age of four and a half unable to speak a word of English' would say that 'we progressed [in English] slowly but well'. In 1889 the dominance of the Gaelic language in South Uist looked assured. Even its most ardent supporters could afford to be complacent. They had thousands of reasons for believing that Gaelic would continue to be the first language of the Outer Hebrides, no matter what was taught in the schools. Gaelic was not forbidden in Garrynamonie School: the youngest children were taught and tested in it until they could take lessons from Mr Rea, and during the winter months evening classes in Gaelic literacy were conducted at the school. In circumstances where 'Gaelic was the sole language talked among the people of the island', teaching their children in English could be justified as giving them fluency in an extra language, rather than replacing one with the other.

The new teacher took a candle up uncarpeted stairs to 'a barely furnished room' where he slept 'in a small, clean bed . . . of Spartan hardness'.

They breakfasted next morning on 'oatmeal porridge and milk, salted herring, newly made scones, oatcake and weak tea'. Father Allan demonstrated to his hesitant guest how 'a little of the hot porridge was taken in a large spoon which was then dipped into the cold milk, and porridge and milk then placed in the mouth'. They walked south to the school at Garrynamonie on a clear, sunny, breezy morning, with the hills on their left and the machair, dunes and ocean on their right, stopping to help three men pull a cow out of a peat bog.

On the following Sunday, the first of 1890, Frederick Rea attended Mass at St Peter's Church in Daliburgh.

As Father Allan had to say the eleven o'clock Mass, of course he was fasting. From before ten o'clock I could see figures, single or in groups, approaching in a leisurely manner from all directions, as far as the eye could reach; some were seen on the road, some crossing boggy ground, but all walking, although I had previously seen many on shaggy ponies, riding bareback. As they arrived in the vicinity of the church the men stopped, resting in groups against walls, or on rocks, evidently engaged in conversation. The women, mostly wrapped in plaid shawls, with a smaller one over their heads and tied tightly at the back of the neck, entered at the paddock gate, steadily advanced up the road and entered the church without pause.

Eleven o'clock arrived and passed, Father Allan went occasionally to the window, and then returned to his chair, saying that he could see more coming in the distance. It was nearer twelve o'clock than eleven before he gave the order for the bell – one salvaged from a wrecked ship – to be rung. Explaining the delay he said: 'Some of them have to come a long way, and not many have clocks, so I do not ring the bell till all have gathered.'

Afterwards I learnt that some came from an island called Eriskay by boat to the other side of the hills, and walked six to eight miles to hear Mass.

The interior of the church looked very bare – small pictures of the Stations of the Cross being the only ornaments – but it was full, men on one side and women on the other. The people worshipped with great decorum and devotion. The language of the Mass, being in Latin, was the same as in the city I had left. I realised the value of this to one away from his native land. The concluding prayers were said in Gaelic, which sounded very strange to me.

Over the following years the English head teacher at Garrynamonie and the Lochaber priest at Daliburgh came to know each other well. Frederick Rea saw Father Allan MacDonald conduct a burial service at the walled cemetery on the open machair. The priest arrived while the grave was being dug by men with 'faces showing no other emotion than that of a quiet serious attention'. When the coffin had been lowered, Father Allan 'assumed a stole, stepped to the side of the grave and recited the beautiful service for the burial of the dead, ending with sprinkling on the coffin lid the holy water from a small bottle which he had brought with him.' Then the men stepped forward one at a time to look respectfully into the grave before retiring to a short distance away. When the dead man's son had gently sprinkled the first spadeful of earth onto the coffin they all stepped forward again, took the spade from the youth and filled in the grave.

The teacher saw the priest at a South Uist wedding. Having conducted the ceremony in St Peter's Church, Father Allan brought the small wedding party into his kitchen. There stood the bride and groom, the bridesmaid and best man, a young piper carrying his instrument, Father Allan, Father Allan's housekeeper and Frederick Rea. The bride and bridesmaid 'wore subdued-coloured dresses and looked very demure, while the men were bright and smiling – all wore sprigs of artificial orange blossom'. A wine glass brimming with neat whisky was handed round, at which everybody sipped but the groom, the best man and the piper, who each emptied the glass at a gulp. 'All this was done with such seriousness and decorum, and in such grave silence . . .'

Then the piper began to play in the kitchen, the bridegroom took the bridesmaid to one side and 'the bride took the orange-blossom from her hair, advanced to me and fixed it in my coat while the others clapped and laughingly told me that I could not refuse the dance'. After two reels there was the sound of many voices outside and the bridal party left to join their friends and relatives, 'headed by the piper playing a march and escorted on their way with a group of people carrying lighted torches. At intervals one or another of these stepped aside and fired a gun over the head of the rest . . .'

Frederick Rea was outside the Daliburgh priest's house one morning to witness the astonishing arrival of an emissary from Father Allan's old friend John Mackintosh, who was settled in the central parish of South Uist.

Along the road came at full gallop a large white horse with a young woman seated sideways on its back ... she slid easily to the ground almost before it came to a standstill. I noted she had ridden without saddle or bridle.

After a rapid conversation [with Father Allan] in Gaelic, she put her foot on the bar of the gate, sprang lightly to the back of the horse which immediately started off at full gallop on receiving a slap from its rider. It transpired that she had come with some important message from the priest of Bornish, the next parish eight miles away. On my speaking of her remarkable riding [Father Allan] exclaimed: 'Oh, that's nothing', as if it were not worthy of comment.

Father John Mackintosh had made himself at home in South Uist. His love of shinty, shooting and fishing were rewarded in the island. His love of riding, which was obviously shared with the young men and women of his parish, had led to the Uist people giving their Bornish priest the affectionate nickname 'Sagart Mor nan Each', or the Big Priest of the Horses. Father John was well adapted to Bornish. The post-harvest Michaelmas sporting events were held within his parish at Aird Michael. His house and church were surrounded by freshwater lochs jumping with fish.*

The young Uist and Barra priests occasionally assembled in John Mackintosh's congenial house at Bornish. On one occasion they held a retreat there under the supervision of a Jesuit from England. Father John killed a sheep for provisions. They dined off it on the first evening, but on the following morning he had to announce that a dog had got in during the night and made off with the mutton. 'What will we do?'

'We'll do fine with salt herring and potatoes.'

'I'm not troubling myself about you. What will the Englishman do?'

---

* Father Michael MacDonald of South Uist said in 2010, 'Father John MacKintosh had a huge reputation in Bornish parish not least because he won land for the Stoneybridge crofters from the Ormiclate farm under the Congested Districts scheme'.

The English Jesuit professed himself happy with fish, but he did wonder about the brown, peaty water – 'Surely you'll all be poisoned.'

'Och – it's a grand water, this! Meat and drink both. It's a very nourishing water!'

They also drank Spanish wine, probably imported from the Boecillo vineyard of their alma mater. They were 'as jolly as schoolboys when they get together ... I've laughed so much sometimes I've had to go outside and knock my head against the wall,' Father Allan said.

Frederick Rea visited John Mackintosh at the priest's house in Bornish, which he shared with his two younger sisters. Rea passed a paddock containing 'a mettlesome black horse' and entered a porch full of sporting guns and fishing rods. The teacher was then stopped in his tracks by the appearance in a doorway of an immense dog with 'eyes almost level with mine ... a huge head with heavy black drooping lips, long dark-tawny powerful body, and great paws'. They stared at each other motionlessly until 'I heard firm heavy steps in the hall; a stalwart black-bearded man in clerical dress appeared in the porch.

'"Back, Hamlet," he said to the dog ...'

The two men took tea together in Father John's spacious, book-lined 'library and sitting-room combined'. Afterwards as they sat smoking, Frederick Rea mentioned the game of chess.

'My host sprang to his feet and exclaimed: "Chess! Do you play chess?" Father John produced a chess board and pulled two chairs up to the table. "Oh! I am so glad," he said. "I have not had a game of chess since I came to the Isles."'

They played until 2.00 a.m. Then after breakfast on the following morning they played chess again, throughout the day and evening, 'only snatching a hasty dinner and tea so as to return the more quickly to our game'. They played into the night, went to bed, got up and went immediately back to the board. 'We had had about three days of chess and agreed that I must return home the next day. I felt really happy that I had been able to help my host to indulge in the intellectual game of playing chess.'

It seems from that conversation that Father Allan MacDonald, Father John's former schoolmate and college friend, did not play chess. He had other passions. They were not exclusively intellectual. Although never so robust an outdoorsman as John Mackintosh – who could not, for instance, manage to interest his old friend in shooting – Allan MacDonald kept his large frame fit. He enjoyed walking and climbing in the hills of South Uist. He refused a carriage or a horse and walked everywhere. 'Whatever the distance or the state of the weather,' said Frederick Rea, 'on sick-call visits or other missions, he always walked, disdaining any aid but that of his own legs.' When he crossed the sound from South Uist to celebrate Mass in Eriskay, he insisted on taking the tiller of the small sailing skiff from its experienced owner. On at least one such occasion he ran the boat onto a sandbank, took off his boots and socks and jumped overboard to push it into deep water.

He fished with rod and line in the sea and in the freshwater lochs, particularly favouring Loch Dun na Cille between Daliburgh and Garrynamonie. Frederick Rea remembered unsuccessfully fishing a Uist loch one evening, when 'I saw a tall dark figure leaving the road, crossing the rough ground, and coming towards us.' Father Allan listened to Rea regretting the absence of bites, told the Englishman to stay where he was, strode off and 'returned with an enormous clumsy-looking rod about eighteen feet in length'. He then led Rea a short distance to another small loch with an island in the middle, scraped several bright red worms out from under stones and stored them in moss in a tobacco tin. The priest baited his hook and 'gave a mighty sweep with his rod and dropped the bait near the island. Almost immediately it was taken and he hauled out a nice trout about a couple of pounds ...' Having shown the way, Father Allan put a cork float on his line, cast it out again, sat down, lit his pipe and watched judiciously as Rea proceeded to catch his own fish.

Allan MacDonald loved music. 'He often invited different pipers to his house to play for him,' said Frederick Rea. 'He was a typical Highlander; he told me that he was born at the foot of Ben Nevis so his love of the traditional pipes was not to be wondered at. I noted how his eyes lighted up at the music of a strathspey, and, at a pibroch, his rugged weather-beaten countenance became suffused with colour and he drew himself to his full six feet height at its warlike strains.' He was known, another acquaintance was told, for remonstrating with the piper at a wedding dance – 'Suas e!' – if the tempo fell.

He was a linguist. Allan MacDonald was fluent in five languages: English, Scottish Gaelic, Latin, French and Spanish. He had also a workable knowledge of Irish Gaelic and Basque, the latter brought back from his time in Spain, where he had met some of the famously amiable Basque priests – who would not have found it difficult to interest Allan MacDonald in an ancient minority language surviving against the odds in the far north of a large European country.

He was an avid reader and a cultivated conversationalist. Sitting in one armchair with his long legs stretched out and resting on another, an American visitor would remember him,

> ... a pipe in his mouth, a good fire and a listener before him, truly here was a man that needed no drawing out. Yet he himself could listen – none better, and a quicker at the up-take never was. Say what you would, you'd get no blank looks from the priest ...
>
> Whitman – Whittier – Longfellow – most of our American classics he'd dipped into first or last: never tired to hear about 'the States' ... 'I'm so interested in those po' whites' I remember him saying after I'd been mentioning our Southern mountaineers ... 'A deep scholar,' some have called him ... He himself used to say, he never broke his head studying. The truth lay between the two, I take it, for he seemed to know more or less of most things you could mention ...

His house, Frederick Rea would report, 'was sparsely furnished with the sole exception of one wall of his sitting room which was entirely occupied by his books carefully arranged on the shelves of a huge bookcase reaching from floor to ceiling and end to end of the wall'. When Allan MacDonald's stipend – which would never be more than £120 a year – exhausted itself, he felt the lack of fresh reading material most keenly. 'At present I have nothing to my credit,' he told his diary at the end of December 1897, 'and some pounds of debt, and I lived as frugally as I could and I didn't buy a book during the year, though I was forced to let slip opportunities of buying desirable books at reasonably reduced prices. Without books, without company . . . I feel solitary, and find myself to a certain extent left painfully alone and poised somewhere in vacuity.'

And still there was unpaid community work to be done which, it seemed, only the representatives of the Church were prepared to undertake. In December 1886 the fishermen of Eriskay held a meeting at which they agreed to apply to the Scottish Fishery Board for loans 'in order to purchase larger boats and better gear'. They requested Father Allan MacDonald to present their case to the Board.

He picked up that cause and pursued it tirelessly for years to come. When the Fishery Board or its equivalent in the grant-and-loan field, the Congested Districts Board, were dilatory in responding – as they frequently were, being reluctant to assess claims from such distant quarters – or when they failed to meet his expectations, he took it to the House of Commons. Twenty years later, in 1904, Allan MacDonald was still relentlessly pressing the case of South Uist and Eriskay fishermen to civil servants and parliamentarians. He wrote in May of that year to Thomas Dewar, the Liberal Inverness-shire Member of Parliament (and heir to the Dewar's whisky fortune):

The Congested Districts Board are to give mackerel nets only to a few boats. I sent a list of fourteen boats from Eriskay. Only three boats get nets, and of twenty-two in Uist only five get nets, and instead of giving six nets to a boat these few selected get for each boat nine pieces and all the rest none.

Now, I think this is iniquitous, as the poor people were so full of expectation, now blasted completely away. Several came in their extremity to me to write to you strongly on the point. This winter was behind in supplying wreck driftware for their land; but a good supply came lately, to which they gave their attention. Now with the wet weather they cannot get along with their tillage, which predicts a late and poor harvest; add to that no chance of fishing (what they look forward to) mackerel, and it makes the life of our unfortunate crofter fishermen a very gloomy one indeed. Can anything be done to explain the condition to the Government?

In regard to herring nets for the Eriskay fishermen, will the authorities not listen to plain facts? This morning an Eriskay boat came into the Loch with four crans* of herrings, the first for the season. They report good appearance, but that boat and others from Eriskay [have] fifteen to twenty nets in all when they ought to have at least forty. How is it possible to make headway? They have the boats, the experience and the will, I can assure you, but lack nets as I explained to you. If any accident happens, and they lose some nets they will be stranded. Now would be the time to encourage them, and not when they are totally stranded.

I can recommend the Eriskay fishermen for pluck as sailors and fishermen; given the material they can fish aside anyone, and yet the Government for the Irish Vote will supply the Irish with boats, gear, and instructors, and leave the unfortunate Eriskay fishermen to their fate; and a net or two to each man (five in a boat) would be a great help. Will this be denied them when the season promises good?

---

* A cran is a Scottish measurement of fresh herring, sufficient to fill a 37½ gallon container, or box. The Eriskay boat's four crans would have amounted to around 3,000 fish.

'Why', Thomas Dewar demanded of his fellow MPs, 'should the local priest or local merchant or Member of Parliament have to apply to the Board? It is the duty of the Board to find out these cases and apply a remedy.'

There was no hospital in South Uist. The gravely sick of the island had to be sent on the long sea crossing to Oban, an option which was practically available only to the small bourgeoisie. Everybody else was cared for at home, visited by the doctor and the priest, and recovered or died in their own beds.

Allan MacDonald and John Mackintosh both knew that the recently erected St Columba's Cathedral on the esplanade at Oban had been subsidised by the unofficial patron of the diocese, the Marquess of Bute. John Patrick Crichton-Stuart, the third Marquess of Bute, had been received into the Catholic Church at the age of 20 in 1868. He was colossally wealthy, with vast estates and extensive industrial interests. The Marquess was also a busy philanthropist, with a particular interest in architecture. He commissioned and restored chapels, castles and abbeys all over Britain. The two Uist priests suggested that Bute might be approached to help build a cottage hospital in the island. He was, and he did.

The Hospital of the Sacred Heart was built with money from the Marquess of Bute in Father Allan's parish, on the road to Lochboisdale out of Daliburgh, in the early 1890s. A solid, four-square, unpretentious building which nonetheless towered over the surrounding landscape, crofts and cottages, it was the work of a celebrated local stonemason, Iain 'Clachair' Campbell from South Lochboisdale, who had trained in Mallaig and left his buildings all over the west coast. Its large ground floor contained the beds and medical equipment; its upper floor contained a chapel and a convent for the nuns who would operate the hospital. The creation of the Hospital of the Sacred Heart, which would become popularly known as the Bute Hospital, was one of the most significant practical improvements ever made to the quality of life of ordinary Uist people.

Allan MacDonald's growing fascination with the culture of South Uist led him to explore its prehistory. He became an amateur archaeologist. Frederick Rea noticed in the Daliburgh priest's house 'stone and bone combs, pins, stone spear and axe heads and other things he had found among the sands of the machair, relics, he said, of the Stone Age'. Father Allan energetically explored the 'primitive habitations' of the island. He sieved through the middens of ancient sites and conjectured – correctly – that the limpets and other shells found there indicated a civilisation which predated the Norse invasions, 'as the abler [Viking] seamen would have been independent of such humble landlubbers' food'.

A hint of the extent of Allan MacDonald's archaeological investigations in South Uist was suggested by the notes that he gave to Ada Goodrich-Freer, who duly published them in one of her own books.

Just to the east of Garrynamonie, south of Daliburgh, was a chambered cairn called Dun Trossary. Father Allan learned that some masons had, while laying the foundations of a new house there, accidentally uncovered the antique flooring, which was of clay laid upon peat. He was told that an underground dwelling had been discovered at an *airigh*, or summer grazing, in the island 20 years earlier. It was

> unfortunately destroyed to furnish stones for building a store for the local merchant. A mason who was present at its destruction describes it as about thirty feet long, five wide, and four high. It was not floored with stone, and he could not say if both ends were open. Some fragments of clay pots were found, and a quantity of limpet shells. A large stone slab showed traces of fire, and the roof was of stone covered over with earth.

At South Glendale, where the hills of South Uist ran down towards the Sound of Eriskay, 'there was found a stone of oblong shape with a cavity in it large enough to hold a quart. It was placed in the wall of Ferguson's shearing-house half in and half out, so as to hold oil and serve as a lamp for the sheep-shearers. It was put in by a mason at Loch Boisdale named Donald Campbell.'

Six miles north-east of Daliburgh, between the 1,000-foot east-coast hills of Stulabhal and Triuirebheinn – 'a spot of quite exceptional beauty in South Uist' – sat a small, round lochan. This was said, Father Allan MacDonald told Ada Goodrich-Freer

> . . . to be the site of the last battle fought in Uist between the natives and the Lochlannaich (Vikings). Close by are remains of peculiar character. There is an artificial cavern about twenty-five feet long and varying in width from two feet at the entrance to five and a half at the end. The height too is variable, the general outline of the cavern being of the shape of the letter S. There are no signs of fire within. It is built regularly, but without lime, and there are two large cairns at the spot, now somewhat scattered. Two small stone pillars beside the lake are called Carragh a bhroin, the Pillar of Sorrow, so called, says tradition, because the wounded were brought here. It is alleged too, that after the battle the combatants cast their arms into the lake, hence called the Lake of Arms to this day.

As well as souterrains, standing stones and axe-heads, Father Allan naturally investigated the origins of the Celtic Church in Uist. In the east coast hills, he discovered, 'there is a stone known as the Rock of Columcille, upon which every wayfarer seats himself before passing on'. That was clearly at one time a place of burial or worship: the word 'Columcille' is Gaelic for St Columba. He was consequently driven to identify the old Christian dedications, the original consecrated buildings or altars in Uist as having been at Kilbride, Kilphedar, Kildonan, Kilchoinnich, Aird Michael,

Kilvanan, Kilaulay and the graveyard called Cladh Chaluim Chille.*

It all led back to the motherlode of South Uist folklore. 'Never call a man a fool,' Father Alexander Campbell had advised Father Allan MacDonald, 'because he believes what isn't likely.' It was good advice to a Catholic priest, and he took it. Allan MacDonald began seriously to collect Uist folklore and Gaelic idiom in around 1887, when he had been in the Hebrides for three years. John Lorne Campbell, who knew several of Father Allan's friends and contemporaries personally, wrote that 'once he was settled in and had mastered the local Gaelic dialect, Fr Allan kept a series of note-books in which he jotted down whatever of interest he heard and had time to record, for instance, when spending nights away from home after sick calls to remote places'.

In March 1892 a man named William MacKenzie rose to give an address to the Gaelic Society of Inverness. William MacKenzie had, as a precocious teenaged schoolboy 20 years earlier, helped to establish the society, and he was its secretary between 1876 and 1886. The society was supportive of the crofters' cause during the land struggles which led to the Napier Commission hearings and the subsequent Crofters' Act. Following the passing of that Act in 1886 a Crofters Commission was established. Effectively a civil land court, its job was to police and administer the Crofters' Act by fixing fair rents, adjudicating rent revisions and settling other disputes between landowners and their crofting tenantry. MacKenzie resigned from the secretariat of the Gaelic Society of Inverness and became the full-time secretary of the Crofters Commission.

His new job caused him to travel all over the Highlands and Islands. It presented him with an ideal opportunity to pursue his

---

* Although there is no evidence of Columba ever visiting the Uists, 'After thirteen hundred years you find his name everywhere,' Allan MacDonald once said. 'If the people were wanting a boy, and one happens along without being sent for, they say, "Columcille has sent me a boy".'

interests in the Gaelic language and folklore. When in South Uist, MacKenzie soon fell in with the Daliburgh priest who, he was pleased to learn, shared those very interests.

So when in 1892 its former secretary returned to the Gaelic Society of Inverness to present a long essay on 'Gaelic Incantations, Charms and Blessings in the Hebrides', William MacKenzie on three separate occasions in the course of his address thanked Father Allan MacDonald of Daliburgh in South Uist, 'a gentleman to whom I am indebted for much information in connection with this paper'.

The information thus gleaned was extraordinary. William MacKenzie told of the ancient divination known as the 'frith', which was

... not yet an institution of the past in some of the Outer Islands, and when the fate of absent ones is causing friends anxiety, or when it is uncertain whether the illness of men or of the lower animals may speedily pass away or terminate fatally, a Frith is made. A Frith may be made at any time; but the first Monday of the quarter – *a' chiad Di-luain de'n Raithe* – is considered the most auspicious.

The mode of making the Frith is as follows:

In the morning the Ave Maria, or *Beannachadh Moire*, is said thus –

> *Beannaichear dhut, a Mhoire,*
> *Tha thu lan dhe na grasan;*
> *Tha 'n Tighearna maille riut;*
> *'S beannuichte thu measg nam ban;*
> *'S beannaichte toradh do bhronn – Iosa.*
> *A Naomh Mhoire – 'Mhathair Dhe –*
> *Guidh air ar son-ne, na peacaich,*
> *A nis agus aig uair ar bais – Amen.*

After repeating the Ave, the person proceeds with closed eyes to the door. On reaching the maide-buinn, or door-step, he opens his eyes, and if he sees the Cross (Crois Chriosda), although it were only made with two straws lying across each other, it is a sign that all will be well. On getting outside, he proceeds round the house sunwise (deiseal), repeating [an] Incantation . . .

The Incantation finished, the person looks forth over the country, and by the auguries or omens which meet the eye he divines what will be the fate of the man or animal for whom the Frith is being made – whether the absent one, about whom nothing is known, is in life, and well; or whether the sick man or beast at home will recover from his ailment. Subjoined is a list of objects with their significance . . .

A man coming towards you . . . An excellent sign.

A cock looking towards you . . . Also an excellent sign.

A man standing . . . Sign of a sick man recovering and casting off illness.

A man lying down . . . Sickness; continued illness.

A beast lying down . . . Ominous – sickness; continued illness; death.

A beast rising up . . . Sign of a man recovering and throwing off illness.

A bird on the wing . . . A good sign.

A bird on the wing coming to you . . . Sign of a letter coming.

A woman seen standing . . . A bad sign – such as death, or some untoward event.

And so on. The survival of those Celtic pagan auguries through adoption by a pragmatic Christianity into the age of the Royal Mail ('A bird on the wing coming to you . . . Sign of a letter coming') was a source of endless interest to a curious intellectual who would live to read of humans flying aeroplanes. Allan MacDonald also gave William MacKenzie the local verse 'Sloinneadh Brighde, muime Chriosd' ('The Genealogy of St Bridget, foster-mother of Christ'), a projection of Uist fascination with personal patrimony onto the Holy Family:

Father Allan MacDonald of Eriskay (National Trust for Scotland)

Blairs Seminary on Deeside: the daunting pile to which Allan MacDonald travelled at the age of 11 in 1871.

A group of pupils at Blairs in 1863, eight years before Allan MacDonald arrived there. Seated on the left is Reverend David MacDonald, the dashing young professor who as Rector 'Don David' would have a great influence on Allan MacDonald at the Scots College in Valladolid 13 years later.

Allan with some fellow students in Valladolid in about 1878, when he was 19 years old. He is seated second from the left in the front row. Immediately to his right at the end of the row is James Chisholm, who would work in Barra during Allan MacDonald's time in South Uist and Eriskay. Duncan MacQueen from Kintail is second from the left in the middle row, and Donald MacLellan from South Uist is second from the right in the front row.

The Lord of the Isles: Father Allan at sea in oilskins, probably crossing between South Uist and Eriskay. (W.B. Blaikie, reproduced by kind permission of D.R. Killpatrick)

'A fine player of shinty and a cattleman': Sagart Mor nan Each, Father John Mackintosh of Bornish, Allan MacDonald's lifelong colleague and friend.

Father George Rigg of Daliburgh, the Gaelic speaking, football-playing son of a Shropshire mother and a Lowland father whose death left Allan MacDonald in 'a world without sun'.

'The stand on which to place the missal was a roughly-shaped piece of rock, while the other accessories were almost as primitive. Father Allan took a small portable altar-stone . . .' The old St Michael's Church in Eriskay, with Father Allan sitting on a rock before it. (W.B. Blaikie, reproduced by kind permission of D.R. Killpatrick)

'It is probable that nothing could have added to the original purity of St Michael's Church in Eriskay when it was completed in 1903.' The new St Michael's Church in Eriskay. The priest's house, which had been built and occupied ten years earlier, is behind it. (National Trust for Scotland)

Island and mainland clergymen from the Diocese of Argyll and the Isles at the consecration of the new St Michael's Church in May 1903. At the centre of the back row stands Bishop George Smith from the Enzie, with Allan MacDonald immediately to his left. (National Trust for Scotland)

'It was on Sunday mornings that the whole island turned out. Then a long procession of women, young and old, of bairns, and of great, dark, brawny men, might be seen climbing up the hill, as Father Allan came out of his presbytery, and himself tolled the bell which called them to worship.'
(National Museums Scotland)

A group of Eriskay women waulking tweed and singing their worksongs, as their priest looks on, all staged for the camera of Walter Blaikie in 1898.
(W.B. Blaikie, reproduced by kind permission of D.R. Killpatrick)

The High Priest. Father Allan MacDonald as his congregation knew him, at the age of 39 in 1898. (W.B. Blaikie, reproduced by kind permission of D.R. Killpatrick)

Brighdhe nighean Dughaill Duinn,
'Ic Aoidh, 'ic Arta, 'ic Cuinn.
Gach la is gach oidhche
Ni mi cuimhneachadh air sloinneadh Brighde.

(St Bridget, the daughter of Dughall Donn,
Son of Hugh, son of Arthur, son of Conn.
Each day and each night
I will meditate on the genealogy of St Bridget.)

'Father Allan MacDonald's Collection', as William MacKenzie labelled it, was then just a few years old. He had quickly discovered, to his unfathomable delight, that he had been born in time to experience in South Uist Alexander Carmichael's assertion that

> Perhaps no people had a fuller ritual of song and story, of secular rite and religious ceremony, than the Highlanders. Mirth and music, song and dance, tale and poem, pervaded their lives, as electricity pervades the air. Religion, pagan or Christian, or both combined, permeated everything – blending and shading into one another like the iridescent colours of the rainbow. The people were sympathetic and synthetic, unable to see and careless to know where the secular began and the religious ended – an admirable union of elements in life for those who have lived it so truly and intensely as the Celtic races everywhere have done, and none more truly or more intensely than the ill-understood and so-called illiterate Highlanders of Scotland.

That rainbow culture certainly was all-pervasive. The South Uist School Board's attendance officer, Donald MacCormick, was a middle-aged native of the island who had travelled widely in his younger years and returned as the embodiment of a modern man. Donald MacCormick had a 'logical critical view on life in general'. He was well-read, possessed a 'thoroughly independent outlook' and was much valued for his common-sensical judgement of 'current politics and prominent men'. Donald MacCormick also believed unshakeably, from first-hand experience, in the power and presence of second sight. He made a collection of Gaelic proverbs and waulking songs,* which he shared with Father Allan MacDonald. In such an environment, in the company of such people, the Daliburgh priest's excavations were all but inevitable.

He noted stories, songs, phrases and items from the rich Uist lexicon. In 1889 Father Allan made his first unique contribution to what Alexander Carmichael called the Gaelic 'ritual of song and story, of secular rite and religious ceremony'. He prepared a short Gaelic hymnal, which included a commentary on the antiphonic, or sung Mass in the language of the Highlands and Islands.

That was a progressive initiative for a nineteenth-century Catholic priest to take. While Hebridean priests might, and did, sermonise and hear confessions in Gaelic, for one and a half millennia the international language of the Roman Missal had been Latin. It is unlikely that even the founding saints of the Celtic Church in Ireland and western Scotland, 1,500 years earlier, had delivered the liturgy in any other language. For all the Ionan abbots' famous quarrels with Rome about the date of Easter and the shape of the tonsure, there is no record or rumour of them ever rejecting Latin.

Allan MacDonald did not reject Latin either; he continued to say Mass in it. But instead of delivering an explanatory commentary in English, as was commonplace elsewhere in Britain, he explicated in Gaelic. 'Fr Allan's commentary on the Mass is brilliant,' said a twenty-first-century Hebridean priest, 'as a

---

* 'Waulking' or fulling lengths of tweed by hand, was a traditional female activity in the Hebrides, and numerous Gaelic shanties had evolved to accompany it. The waulking process involved a group of women sitting facing each other across a table, upon which the length of cloth would be stretched and pounded until its impurities had been removed and it had achieved a fuller consistency. The rhythmic pushing and thumping of waulking provided a natural percussion to a variety of songs and chants

catechetical and devotional "tool" in the language of the people. He was constantly seeking new ways to teach the eternal truths.'

The millennial attachment of the western Latin Church to the language of the See of St Peter would not be weakened until the Second Ecumenical Council of the Vatican of 1962–65. Among the reforms instituted by Vatican Two was an article providing that the Mass could henceforth be said and sung in the vernacular of the congregation. From the middle of the 1960s onwards it was no longer obligatory for Roman Catholic priests in every corner of the earth to deliver the whole of the liturgy in the 'universal language' of the Church. They could use Latin or the local vernacular. In the Hebrides that meant Latin or Gaelic.

Eighty years earlier the Gaelic commentary was more of a visionary than a rebellious act on the part of the Daliburgh priest. But it is possible to read two characteristic tensions into Allan MacDonald's vernacular commentary on the Mass. It was his latter-day assertion of the proud autonomy of the old Celtic Church. And it was a small internal skirmish between his two great loyalties and loves: the Gaelic language and the Roman Catholic Church – a skirmish which, on that occasion, Gaelic won.

Such work in the heartlands of Gaelic language and culture quickly attracted the attention of the wide circle of late Victorian Celtic folklorists and revivalists. William MacKenzie of the Gaelic Society of Inverness was only one of many to be drawn to the intelligent, witty and sensitive man whom his people knew formally as Maighstir Ailean, and the visiting mainlanders as Father Allan. Through no volition of his own, and eventually at some unquantifiable cost to his health, a legend began to be cultivated around the tall young priest at Daliburgh.

In 1892 a 26-year-old scholar named George Henderson visited South Uist. Henderson came from Kiltarlity, a rural parish 12 miles west of Inverness. When he was a boy, over 80 per cent of the people of Kiltarlity spoke Gaelic, so he was probably a native speaker of the language. He was certainly fluent by the late 1880s, when he graduated from Edinburgh University in English Literature, Philosophy and Celtic and became the university's Master of Arts examiner in Celtic Studies. The Reverend Dr George Henderson later became a Bachelor of Literature at Jesus College, Oxford, for his work on Scottish Gaelic dialects. He was also a Doctor of Philosophy at Vienna, a Church of Scotland minister, a collector of folksongs and a lecturer in Gaelic at Glasgow University. But in the early winter of 1892 he was merely a 'shy, likeable, unpretentious' young man who sat down late one night in the priest's house at Daliburgh and wrote to his distinguished friend Alexander Carmichael.

> Though I should stay months here busy as a House of Commons' Clerk, I should find my hands fully occupied. Father Macdonald I like exceedingly; we are glad good friends and sit and jaunt about as suits us. I could not desire a more congenial companion; and so far as Celtic matters are concerned his taste is high and refined, while his knowledge is wide and accurate. I like the mind and the man and everybody who knows him is bound to do the same.

Having mentioned that his host was shortly to take him to Eriskay, George Henderson then offered Carmichael an echo of some of his political conversations with Father Allan MacDonald. 'Almost all I know of the islanders redounds to their credit,' he wrote. 'Fancy persons such as these forced to starvation point by donkeys and brutes of hireling superiors . . . The big farms need to be broken up and nobody needs speak of emigration of any sort till what land we have is divided among the people.'

On Boxing Day 1892 Henderson, having reluctantly left South Uist, wrote again to Carmichael from Oban. His expedition to the island, he said, had been fruitful beyond expectation.

Fr Allan is to do the Feinn Saga for me; he will transcribe the Gaelic version of 'The Raising of the Feinn' so that the incidents may be kept in sequence ... There is a first class reciter in Eriska from whom no one ever took down a word, and Iain Taillear at Dalibrog from whom nobody ever took down a word ... Between MSS given me by Fr Allan of songs by Dr Macdonnell who was at Plockton, and various Catholic pieces of merit, I have a number of songs by living poets ...

Just as William MacKenzie would not have uncovered the incantations of the frith or the Genealogy of St Bridget without Allan MacDonald's unstinting help, so the young George Henderson would have floundered on his own in South Uist. A man just a little older than they, with a full-time vocation to pursue, who had nonetheless found the time and energy to build his own unparalleled collection of song, legend and lore, was happy to give it all away. If his gifts helped to build the reputations and line the pockets of other men and women, as they frequently did, he was indifferent to the fact. Many folklorists shared some of their material. Only one of them dispensed it all freely to each and every curious visitor, without asking for as much as a printed acknowledgement. Some would use Father Allan's generosity better than others, and one at least would abuse it. He mildly resented the instance of minor abuse from Ada Goodrich-Freer, chiefly because his friends took offence at her presumption, but it is difficult to detect elsewhere a moment of animus or regret. He handed over 'Father Allan MacDonald's Collection' for the same simple reason that he had assembled it: his unqualified love of its content. Listening to, wondering at and then recording the syncretic 'Mirth and music, song and dance, tale and poem ... pagan or Christian' of the late nineteenth-century Hebrides had been a greater personal reward than he had ever hoped to find. It was not in his nature, his education or his faith to hoard or to profit from such riches. So long as his people's culture was not corrupted or misrepresented in the retelling, he wanted the world to know of it. He assumed, with illuminating and attractive innocence, that the world in return would offer that kaleidoscopic culture the same love and respect which it had elicited from himself.

At the end of 1893 Father Alexander Campbell died. The man who had introduced the mysteries of South Uist to Father Allan, who had talked and walked the young clergyman through his first priesthood, passed away at noon on a mid-November day. Allan MacDonald was present to minister the last rites. The local doctor, Hugh MacIntyre, diagnosed the cause of Father Campbell's death as chronic bronchitis.* He was 74 years old.

Allan MacDonald himself had passed his thirty-fourth birthday three weeks earlier. To a Victorian he was in middle age. He felt older. He had been in South Uist for almost ten eventful years. He was mentally, physically and emotionally exhausted. In the words of Father Michael MacDonald, the pastoral work of the parish alone 'would have been grinding and unrelenting: up to ninety baptisms a year, the usual round of [daily] Masses, confessions, instructions, marriages, funerals . . .'

There were unsettling changes in other quarters. In July 1892 his patron and friend in Oban, Bishop Angus MacDonald, was elevated to the senior Scottish position, the Archbishopric of St Andrews and Edinburgh. He left behind him in the west Highlands and Islands a posse of young and dedicated priests and new or reconstituted Catholic parishes, churches and schools at Knoydart, Barra, Benbecula, Morar, Canna and in half a dozen other parts of the Gaelic diocese.

Bishop Angus was replaced six months later by George John Smith. Bishop Smith was a 52-year-old priest from the tiny village of Cuttlebrae in north-eastern Morayshire. He was a product of the traditional Catholic community of the Enzie, a

---

* 'Father Campbell does not sleep well on account of asthma', the visiting George Henderson had written to Alexander Carmichael a year earlier.

district which overlapped into Moray from western Banffshire. The Enzie was noted for its ample harvest of priests, regularly delivering more young ordinands than their native north-east could hire. Accordingly, Enzie men filled parishes all across the rest of Scotland. George Smith had served at Rothesay in the south-western island of Bute before being transferred to the Oban see. Although he was not a Gaelic speaker he would have been accommodated in Bute: by the second half of the nineteenth century only a small minority of the people of that island spoke the language, and all but a handful of them also spoke English.

Argyll and the Isles was a different matter. Bishop Smith would govern the diocese for 25 years, until his death early in 1918. During that period he was unable to communicate directly with around half of his parishioners in Benbecula, South Uist, Eriskay and Barra, and with a good many other people elsewhere in the diocese. Whatever they thought of the man himself, Allan MacDonald and his fellow Hebridean priests responded to that deficiency with bewilderment. Father Allan could not help but reflect on the long apprenticeship in Gaelic that he had been obliged to serve before being permitted to enter an island parish. Bishop Angus MacDonald had been known to consider 'a certain [other] priest's Gaelic so poor that he was of little use to the diocese'.

Times were changing in an unfamiliar and uncomfortable fashion. For that reason and others, Allan MacDonald began to consider a move of his own. 'It's time for me to be taking stock,' he wrote in 1892.

Two or three years before Alexander Campbell's death, Frederick Rea accompanied Father Allan on an overnight visit to say Mass and administer the sacraments in the island of Eriskay. It was a journey which, the priest told another visitor, he made from Uist every third week. The two men walked south from Daliburgh and Garrynamonie along the road towards Trossary, where the chambered cairn had been uncovered, and then turned eastward up into the hills. From the summit of their climb they saw beneath them the Sound of Eriskay.

'Below us to the south,' said Rea, 'lay a beautiful wild glen studded with boulders and carpeted with heather, soft grass, and many varieties of fern, among which I recognised the royal fern. The beauty of this sheltered place was enhanced by the fine bright day and the gentle soft air.'

They walked down towards the clear, blue sea with its bed of white sand. Across the shallow sound the low hills of Eriskay floated lazily on the water. They reached 'a large elevated rock, the flat top of which was scorched'.

'This is the priest's point,' said Father Allan, 'and we must light a fire.'

He picked dry grass and ferns from the hillside, and driftwood and crisp, desiccated seaweed from the shore. He lit the fire on the slab of rock. When it was blazing he gathered at the water's edge armfuls of moist, brown tangle and heaped them on the blaze. A plume of dense, black smoke immediately ascended into the air.

Father Allan sat down in a hollow, filled and lit his pipe and said, 'This is the Highlander's glory – with back to the wind and face to the sun'.

Frederick Rea looked around him at the islands and islets which studded the sea between South Uist, Eriskay and Barra. Occasionally Father Allan looked keenly towards Eriskay, and put more damp seaweed on the fire. 'This performance had been repeated several times, when, gazing across again, he sat down with an exclamation of satisfaction. Looking steadily across the sound . . . I could see a column of smoke rising from a high point on the opposite shore. Our signal was answered!'

The priest and the teacher sat back again in the grass, smoked their pipes and waited for their boat. 'Well,' asked Father Allan rhetorically, 'do you want to be back in your city?' Then he sighed and said, 'Ah! God made the country and the deil made the toon.'

A skiff with a red-brown sail tacked across the sound. An old man and a ten-year-old boy helped them aboard. They were put ashore on the rocks at Haun on the north coast of Eriskay. The boy carried their belongings up to the schoolhouse, where the schoolmistress gave them lunch. After eating and digesting they walked up the nearest hill. 'At our feet lay the sound we had crossed, the hills and mountains of our island [South Uist] receding in wonderful graduation of light and shade far into the distance and its white sands gently lapped by the sea. Away to the south-west, past several smaller islands, was Barra . . .'

They scrambled around a cliff-face and made their way to the sandy, western shore of Eriskay, where they sat and watched salmon leaping. Father Allan talked of climbing, and of the cragsmen of the most westerly Hebridean island of St Kilda. 'He himself was born at the foot of Ben Nevis,' Frederick Rea reminded himself, 'and I thought his rugged features and tall powerful figure typified his birthplace.'

After Mass the following morning in the small thatched chapel on the hillside above Coilleag a' Phrionnsa, the sandy bay where Charles Edward Stuart had come ashore almost 150 years earlier, they were sailed back to Uist. The skiff now took them westward through the sound to Polachar, cruising past basking, swimming, rolling and diving seals. 'Look at the rascals,' smiled Father Allan. 'They seem to know that we have no guns.' They landed in South Uist and walked home. When they reached the turning to Garrynamonie, Frederick Rea asked how much their trip had cost, so that he could pay his share.

'Nothing,' said Father Allan.

'But how much did the boatman charge?'

'Charge! He is only too proud to convey me or my friends. Don't you ever offer them money. They would be insulted.'

Later Frederick Rea remembered that, 'My companion rather startled me by adding that it was his ambition to come some day and spend his life among these poor people.'

His ambition was soon realised.

In 1893 Allan MacDonald's health was close to breaking. Despite his 'tall powerful figure' and obsessive energy he had been ailing for some time. Six years earlier, in 1887, Bishop Angus MacDonald had issued an appeal on behalf of his priest. It read:

> Rev. Allan McDonald, besides the Mission of Daliburgh, South Uist, numbering over 1,500 souls, has charge of an outlying district, the Island of Eriskay, separated from the main Island by a stormy channel and having a population of about 400 souls.
>
> His time and strength are more than fully taxed by the care of the principal mission; whilst such occasional attendance as he is able to give to the Eriskay station, though quite inadequate to the wants of the poor people, involves a serious strain on his strength and danger to his health. For the sake of both priest and people therefore the erection of Eriskay into a separate Mission is urgently called for. The present church, a wretched hovel, has been so far improved internally by his zeal, that it will suffice as a temporary arrangement until funds for a more suitable church are forthcoming. But a house for a resident priest is in the first instance needed, and I have authorised and indeed urged Rev. Allan McDonald, to endeavour to collect the necessary funds.

The Eriskay priest's house was built in 1891 on a hilltop at Rubha Ban in the north of the island, above the anchorage at Haun, a mile from the 'wretched hovel' that was the old church. Frederick Rea returned to the island while it was under construction: 'Father Allan ... led us to the site of his new house ... we found it perched on the top of the high rock overlooking the sea, near which he and I had scaled the cliff face. I remarked on the exposed position, but he drew himself to his full height, raised his arms, and exclaimed: 'What could be grander? Exposed to the four winds of heaven!'

Already the building had commenced: the foundations were in the solid rock, some huge stones and boulders, placed in position for walls or lying near, were ready to be roughly dressed. We learned that these poor fishermen of the island were building their priest's house ... with their own hands, making cement from burnt shells and sands, using bulks of wood from the cargoes of timber ships thrown on the sea from wrecked or distressed vessels ...

With an eye on his future recreation, Father Allan had carefully carried with him from Uist a large tin can full of fresh loch water and living trout. He released the fish into Loch Cracabhaig, the only lochan on Eriskay, which conveniently lay a short walk uphill from the old church.

Between 1891 and 1893 the new priest's house on Eriskay provided accommodation to the island's first resident vicar, Father Donald MacKintosh. At the end of 1893 its door was opened by Father Donald's successor, Father Allan MacDonald. He moved into it – and out of Daliburgh – permanently.

He had pushed himself almost to death in South Uist. An island Protestant acquaintance would later tell John Lorne Campbell that as well as being 'the best clergyman South Uist had ever had', Father Allan MacDonald 'did the work of four'. He was so thoroughly absorbed in the priestly duties, political and social activities of his first parish at Daliburgh that he did not realise at the time how close he was to collapse. 'The life I have gone through,' he told his diary afterwards in a spasm of regret, 'I should not like to live through again. It looks more painful in the retrospect than I ever actually felt it ...

God knows that my work was like the work of a machine and perhaps no more meritorious. It went on like a steam engine, careering on wildly without even one truck load of good after it. The machinery was out of gear at last. The ill-regulated enthusiasm wasted the natural strength. The wheels should have been better oiled. My ministry was barren because it was not a ministry resting on prayer. It was too human, as depending on myself and not on God.

At the very end of 1892 he wrote in a Gaelic poem that 'S leir dhomh an cunnart as na tharr mi...' – 'I see the danger from which I've escaped / During the days that have passed me by: / How You have rescued me from death...' His mortal fatigue came close to generating an active dislike of South Uist – of its politics, its divisions, its robust contentions, its fears and insecurities and even of some of its people – which was no suitable state of mind for a clergyman.

Thirteen years after that crisis Father Allan spoke about his sickness in South Uist. He had at first denied his failing health, he said – 'I thought it was lack of fervour that ailed me, and did penance for it.' Then one stormy night as he was making his way home across the machair, he could not catch his breath. 'I thought if I could get off the sand and my feet on the hard ground I could get on. Then if I could get to a wall, I would lie down behind it. But there was no wall, so I kept on. And I don't know why I didn't die, for I didn't want to live.'

The doctor told him to rest. 'And indeed,' Father Allan said, 'my knees were doubling under me when I tried to say Mass.' Feeling that some exercise would do him good he took a crowbar to clear boulders from the ground around St Peter's Church. He had no sooner started than the doctor passed by, stopped and shouted, 'Whatever are you doing there? Don't you know you might be dropping dead any minute?'

'How so?'

'It's your heart that's all wrong.'

'Och – why didn't you tell me that before?'

If he was to live much longer, Allan MacDonald clearly had to leave the most demanding parish in South Uist. He could do so with a clear conscience. The School Board was denominationally representative. A Crofters' Act had passed into law. In 1893 the Hospital of the Sacred Heart opened its doors to the old and infirm of the island. South Uist was a demonstrably happier and freer place in 1893 than it had been in 1884.

Bishop George Smith offered him a town parish on the mainland 'with better living and the company of book-learned men'. He rejected it ('God made the country and the deil made the toon') and asked for Eriskay. Early in January 1894, two months after the death in Daliburgh of Father Alexander Campbell, Father Allan received a presentation clock from his South Uist parishioners. He had already gone to live and work in the new priest's house on Rubha Ban.

7

ERISKAY

‿ 'He was a man about thirty-five years old, tall and spare, beloved of his folk, who called him faithfully behind his back "Lord of the Isles"... A king in some respects, and yet a child in his simplicities.' ‿

Eriskay was one of the few Hebridean islands whose population had increased in the middle of the nineteenth century. Considered by the estate to be agriculturally worthless, it had been used by Colonel John Gordon's agents as a dumping ground for people evicted from elsewhere in the southern Outer Hebrides.

Some of those people were removed to Eriskay from even smaller islands in the Sound of Barra, which could then be used as summer pasture for the estate's tenant farmers' sheep. But most of its men and women were of South Uist descent or had actually been born and raised in the large island to the north. Back in the 1830s and 1840s, said John McCaskill of Eriskay to the Napier Commission, there were just three families on Eriskay, comprising fewer than 30 people.* The population of the island in 1891, shortly before Father Allan MacDonald moved there, was 454 men, women and children.

---

* Other records suggest that in 1841 the population of Eriskay – which was enumerated as part of South Uist – was around 80 people.

'Where did all the others come from?' John McCaskill was asked.

'They came from the opposite side of the sound. They were sent across to the island.'

'From Barra or Uist?'

'From Uist.'

Eriskay is no larger than a toe of South Uist. There are freshwater lochs in Uist which are bigger than the land area of Eriskay. Three miles long from north to south and a mile and a half in breadth, it forms a small oval of stony earth in the open sea between South Uist and Barra. In the 1890s Eriskay had a shop, a post office which was 'just an ordinary thatched house', a postal delivery once a week if the weather allowed, a board school, a church and a priest's house. Unable to plough, because what sparse areas of thin soil there were between Eriskay's rocks had to be turned over by spades or larger hand-held devices known as *cas-chrom*, its people took to the sea. Many of the men went away on naval work; many of the young women became itinerant herring gutters, following the seasonal shoals around the coast of Great Britain. Those who remained fished expertly out of the anchorages at Haun and Acairsaid Mhor in two-masted boats, grew what crops they could, which were mainly potatoes in raised lazy beds, kept a milking cow and reared a few sheep for market in South Uist. '[Eriskay] has no road at all,' Father Odo Blundell would write rosily, 'all traffic, such as carrying peats, etc., being done by creels on the backs of ponies. Fishing is the chief means of livelihood, and this, in addition to the crofts, gives the people all they require. They are indeed remarkably happy and contented. There is no licensed house upon the island . . .'

With the exception of 'two or three' perfectly assimilated Protestant families, including that of the island's storekeeper, Eriskay's 450 people were all Roman Catholics. Four hundred and twenty-four of them, or 93 per cent – effectively every articulate person – spoke Gaelic. One hundred and ninety-four, or 46 per cent of the total population, spoke nothing but Gaelic.

It was a heaven on earth to Father Allan MacDonald. He adored the island of Eriskay and its people. 'Ged a gheibhinn-sa mo thaghadh . . .' he would write in his most famous secular Gaelic poem, 'Eilein na h-Oige', 'The Island of Youth', an exuberant 29-stanza paean to the place in which he left his heart . . .

> Should I even have my choice
> I'd prefer in all of Europe
> A dwelling place beside the wave
> In the lovely Isle of Youth.
> It's bare of foliage, bare of bent-grass,
> Bare of barley-sowing,
> But beautiful for all its bareness
> Is each sod of it to me . . .
>
> In it live the manly people
> Whose ways I find agreeable:
> Of the defects that all men have
> We possess our own fair share,
> But Hanging Back, Stubbornness and Guile,
> Yon epidemic's selfishness –
> Those faults are now completely cast out
> From amongst us across the sea.
>
> Long ago each savage hound
> That heard the Gordon's whistle
> Drove splendid men to the edge of the shore
> Like lambs being rounded up –
> We did not then possess that law
> Which would process our just claim,
> But Providence has come to our rescue
> And turned oppression to our gain.
>
> Folk would often say in derision
> That the island was confined,
> With all of its inhabitants
> In a place like a sheep-fank;

But what has made it all the more lovely,
Each wee bit hill of it and glen,
Is the ring of waves all around it
That keeps unpleasantness outside.

Allan MacDonald found peace and fulfilment in what sounded uncannily like an earlier poet's 'other Eden, demi-paradise, this fortress built by Nature for herself against infection and the hand of war . . . or as a moat defensive to a house, against the envy of less happier lands'. His reciprocated love affair with Eriskay would dominate posterity's version of his life. He would probably have approved.

Although his life and duties after 1894 were devoted to the new insular parish of Eriskay, he was not 'confined' to the place. He had neighbours and colleagues in Barra and South Uist. He occasionally relieved the priests of South Uist. He said Mass as far south as Mingulay. He continued as chairman of the School Board until the April of 1894. And although he had left the parish of Daliburgh, he gained there the dearest of friends.

His successor in South Uist, Father George Rigg, was another exact contemporary of Allan MacDonald. George Rigg was 33 years old when he moved into the vacant Daliburgh priest's house, to be introduced to his new duties by Father Allan, at the end of 1893. He had an unusual background. His father, James Rigg, was a tenant farmer from Castle Douglas in Kirkcudbrightshire, and his mother Eliza was an Englishwoman from Shropshire. His parents therefore were certainly not native Gaelic speakers.

But George himself was born and spent the first seven years of his life in the largest Outer Hebridean island of Lewis. In 1850 James Rigg had transplanted his young family to the Hebrides to run the 200-acre farm at Coll on the east side of Lewis. Eight of James' and Eliza's nine children were born there, including George in 1860. Coll House would, during the Rigg family's occupancy, have maintained an English-speaking interior. But it was a tiny

Anglophone islet in a Gaelic ocean. The rest of the 2,000 people of the fertile district of Coll, Back, Vatisker, Gress, Tong and Tolsta were in the 1850s and 1860s all Gaelic speakers, and over 90 per cent of them knew no English. Young George Rigg learned English at home. But in order to play or associate in any way with the other children of Coll and with the workers on his father's farm, he had to absorb Gaelic. As an infant he would have done so effortlessly.

George Rigg could quickly have lost his Lewis Gaelic if his family had moved from the Hebrides back to Castle Douglas or Shropshire. But in 1867, when George was a schoolboy, James Rigg left Coll Farm for an even larger holding, of 1,500 acres, which was chiefly given over to sheep, at Drimnin on the remote western edge of the Morvern peninsula. If his children (or himself and his wife) required further experience of the Gaelic language they had gone to the right place. The few hundred people in Morvern were almost all Gaelic speakers. George Rigg was once again immersed in the language. Hence the son of a Kirkcudbrightshire father and a Shropshire mother was enabled to work among the Gaelic speakers of South Uist in the 1890s.

In the 1870s, when George Rigg was a teenager, his parents separated. James stayed on the farm in Morvern with two of his single daughters. Eliza moved to Oban with another of the daughters and two of her unmarried sons. One of them was George, who at the age of 20 in 1881 found himself working as a law clerk in the cathedral parish of St Columba, where Bishop Angus MacDonald was establishing his new diocese, and where a year later Allan MacDonald would arrive from Valladolid to begin his vocation in the north-west Highlands and Islands. We do not know if George Rigg first met Allan MacDonald in Oban between 1882 and 1884. It seems likely. They were educated young men of the same age in a small town. They were members of the same modest Catholic congregation, and George Rigg might even then have been considering the priesthood for which he would prepare in Douai and Paris between the middle of the 1880s and 1891.

But we do know that when Father George Rigg became the priest at Daliburgh early in 1894, after three years in Knoydart, he and Father Allan MacDonald of Eriskay instantly became close friends. George Rigg was 'a tall dark man with a gentle kind manner, and I took to him at once,' said Frederick Rea. He had a youthful face, with generous lips and warm, intelligent eyes behind oval rimless spectacles.

'You were so human, angelic,' Father Allan would write of Father George, 'So good-humoured and gentle, / That no scowl would sour your expression . . .'

George Rigg entered South Uist as memorably as he was to depart the island. At Christmas 1893 the schoolteacher Frederick Rea was visited by his two brothers, who were both soldiers and keen footballers. After a kick-around on Garrynamonie machair, which quickly excited the interest of the whole shinty-playing island, they met Father George outside St Peter's Church. The new priest invited the three Englishmen into his house. 'He had heard of our having a football, and said that he had been very fond of the game in his college days; so he made a suggestion that we should bring a team from the south end of the island, and he would provide an eleven to give us a game on the machair after service in church on New Year's Day.'

By New Year's Day 1894, George Rigg had erected goalposts and corner flags on Garrynamonie machair. He selected a Daliburgh/ Lochboisdale/Bornish side from local men augmented by himself, a college student on holiday, an accountant from the bank, two clerks from the Gordon Cathcart estate office and another priest who was almost certainly Father John Mackintosh.

The Reas' team was composed of the three brothers, seven crofters and Father Allan MacDonald in goals – 'right gallantly did he perform'. Refereed firmly by a captain of the Cameron Highlanders who was staying at the Lochboisdale Hotel, and watched by a large crowd, with the three Englishmen up front and the Eriskay priest between the sticks, the south-end team won 3–1. To his certain satisfaction, Father Allan had conceded only one goal to Father George's and Father John's team.

A few months later George Rigg replaced Father Allan on the South Uist School Board. He was soon also elected to the Parish Council and the District Committee of Inverness County Council. Happy to see his former parish in such hands, Allan MacDonald settled into Eriskay.

St Michael's Church in Eriskay had been built in 1852, shortly after the arrival on the island of hundreds of evictees from South Uist and elsewhere. It was no more than a big stone crofthouse, a single-storey rectangle, at first with a thatch and later with a corrugated iron roof, and a crucifix atop each gable end.

> The wooden partitions used to subdivide such [croft] cottages had been removed and the result was a fairly large floor space of beaten earth.
>
> At the far end from the open door [the altar] was a long wooden table, scrubbed spotlessly clean, set crosswise . . . The stand on which to place the missal was a roughly-shaped piece of rock, while the other accessories were almost as primitive. Father Allan took a small portable altar-stone . . . and placed it in the centre of the altar . . .
>
> The people began to troop in, every man in fisherman's garb of blue cloth and blue jersey, the women in plaid shawls [over their shoulders] with small black shawls on their heads. They crowded in together, filling the floor and overflowing to the ground outside, the men on one side, the women on the other. There was the utmost quiet and devotion during the Mass, after which the people trooped out. While the priest was removing his vestments a number of men came in bearing planks which they rested on rocks ranged round the walls. The congregation then returned and sat round on these while some

stood during the time the priest delivered a sermon in Gaelic. After he had given a blessing they all dispersed . . .

Despite Father Allan's amused comment that one of his sermons 'though scriptural evoked sundry yawns!', Eriskay did not lack piety. But it did need a new church. That church could not be built by the diocese. The diocese could in the 1890s barely pay its clergymen. Father Allan and his fellow priests had on rare occasions received stipends of £120 a year. But the impecunious Diocese of Argyll and the Isles became even poorer as the nineteenth century progressed and the twentieth century began. Following a dispute in the 1880s Bishop Angus MacDonald lost the direct benefactions of the Marquess of Bute to diocesan funds, and any possibility of regaining them was dashed with the death of the third Marquess in 1900. John Patrick Crichton-Stuart's heir shared his father's Catholicism but not his philanthropy.

The Diocesan Fund which was collected locally raised only between £100 and £150 a year. It was severely limited by the poverty of most of the Catholics of the west Highlands and Islands and also, as Bishop Angus confided to Father Allan MacDonald in a letter, by the fact that many people imagined that the Croesan riches of the Marquess of Bute were keeping the diocese in wine and roses and absolving anybody else of the need to contribute. Initially, in the late 1870s, Bishop MacDonald had received almost £600 a year from the Association for the Propagation of the Faith at Lyons in France, which had been established in 1822 for the aid of needy Catholic missions throughout the world, but by the 1890s even that contribution had dried up.

In 1892, the first year of his bishopric, George Smith received in Oban a plea from all seven priests in Barra, Eriskay, South Uist and Benbecula. They needed, they said, £100 each a year to do their jobs. But they were getting only £260 between them, or an average of £37 a year per parish. 'They could not ask the people to give more, they said, for they were almost all in debt to the merchants for their food. There was not in all the parishes combined sufficient means to support two priests.'*

So Allan MacDonald lived frugally in the priest's house on Rubha Ban. The chimneys would never cease to smoke, making some rooms either uninhabitable or unheatable at times. He lived there like most bachelors.

> On the walls, tinted robin's-egg-blue, hung some views in Spain and photographs of brother priests, and a coloured print or two, agreeably faded, of Our Lady and the Sacred Heart; and while warming his feet he could look up at the likeness of his late beloved 'Bishop Angus – just a darling bishop!'
>
> All these were of his choosing: so were not the curtains, nor the vases on the side-board, of that uneasy sort that topple over if you touch them; thin glass, backed with quicksilver, painted in crude colours, huge, yet light, as corks. Nor again were the china poodles facing right and left from either side the black marble clock, which had been his 'presentation' when he left Dalibrog.

Apart from his occasional frustration at being unable to afford to buy books, it suited his character and his philosophy to share the privations of his people. His housekeeper when he first arrived was Kate Campbell, a woman in her early 20s from Coilleag, the settlement which lay between the small, old church and the sandy shore. She was a child of simple fishing people. He wished to understand and learn from such women as much as to employ them.

---

* Wrestling once again with the translation of money values between different ages and economies: when Allan MacDonald received a stipend of £120, it gave him the spending power of about £10,000 in 2010. If his stipend fell to £40 a year, he had the modern equivalent of about £3,400. The priests had no housing costs, their heating was donated in the form of peat by their communicants, and food in the Outer Hebrides was cheap when it was not free. They were usually better off than almost all of their parishioners, but compared to their friends in the medical, teaching and other professions they were as poor as . . . church mice.

Due to the infirmity of his mother, Frederick Rea reluctantly left Garrynamonie School and returned to Birmingham in August 1894. He found the priest who had appointed him four years earlier 'the greatest comfort and support to me in my endeavour to act as my duty should lead'. Before catching the southbound steamer, Rea crossed over to see how Father Allan was settling in Eriskay. The priest invited him and the Eriskay schoolmaster to a midday meal on Rubha Ban. Frederick Rea recorded,

> When we duly arrived at the priest's house for dinner, we were surprised to find the table set outside against a wall on the lee side of the house; while a large bucket stood on stones and contained the fire. In explanation our host said, as though it were to himself a matter of small concern: 'I cannot have a fire in any room of the house, for the wind blows down the chimneys and drives the smoke and fire into the room. So we will have dinner here, for you will be cold in the house without a fire.'

After dinner the men took an early afternoon walk. They saw a large boat in full sail crossing to Eriskay from Barra. 'That will be the fishing girls returning from the fisheries on the mainland,' said Father Allan, 'I know they are expected today.' They lit their pipes, and when they looked up again the boat was gone. Every spare vessel in Eriskay was instantly launched to search for the ship or its survivors, with no success. It had capsized in a sudden squall and sunk with all hands and its young passengers. 'I the better understood now the attitude of inimical fear of the sea that I had sensed at times among the people,' said Frederick Rea.

Hebridean life was fragile and death was always close, at home or wherever they travelled to earn money. In August 1887, before Father Allan moved permanently to Eriskay but while it was part of his Daliburgh curacy, three young women from the island, along with two friends from Barra and Lewis, died of German measles – which would later be known as the curable virus rubella – while working as herring gutters and packers at Fraserburgh. They had been sleeping on planks, nine to each small room, in lodgings 'of the most wretched description'. Shortly before Christmas 1894, at the end of Father Allan's first year in the island, an Eriskay boy who was working away from home on a steam lighter boat drowned in the Crinan Canal. Four years later, in his own words:

> Fire at Ludag [signalling for a ferry], dispatched boat. Telegram announcing poor Neil Campbell, Ru Bain's, death on Xmas morning at Arisaig where he went to work on the railway. Death simply from overwork and insufficient food. His large family and his struggle to keep them broke his heart. He was always so cheerful and so industrious, and so pious – a good man who made his soul of it and turned his lot in this world to the best account. When I came to Eriskay first he was the only one who could serve Mass. The poor widow. It was sad breaking the news to her. She has done nothing but faint continuously. Went to see her at night and staid for a couple of hours. Made her some soup. I do hope she will recover poor soul.

Disease and infections regularly visited the islands, where qualified medical support was thin on the ground and modern treatments were beyond most people's means. Father Allan told his diary of another incident in the late 1890s,

> Poor Roderick MacIntyre, Kilpheder was ordered as he had acute pneumonia to have a poultice applied. They envelop the old fellow in porridge without a particle of linen to cover the poultice with, or to protect it from his shirt, and he becomes a mixed up thing, his shirt and body all sticky and damp and cold finally. He spent a night I think this way. No wonder he went to another world quickly.

In 1896 and 1897 the Hebrides were assaulted by the most serious epidemic of typhus in memory. In the ages before antibiotics, epidemic typhus was frequently fatal. This particular attack was almost entirely confined to the islands – there was not a single death from the virus in mainland Inverness-shire, where patients could quickly be isolated in a hospital for infectious diseases – and was especially virulent in Eriskay and South Uist.

The reasons for that were clear to a later age. At the time, in the 1890s and afterwards, blame was attributed to the number of blackhouses in the islands which accommodated people at one end and farm animals at the other. Professor John Percival Day of Dundee was echoing the educated view of his time when he wrote in 1918: 'The South Uist district had still, in 1896, 293 dwelling-houses containing 854 animals, comprising 569 cattle, 204 sheep, and 9 pigs. As a result of the insanitary conditions there was a serious outbreak of typhus fever.'

Insanitary conditions certainly played their part, but the cattle and sheep were innocent. Epidemic typhus is carried by the human body louse. The louse actually catches typhus fever from its human host. It is then transmitted through the louse to other humans. The virus is excreted in the louse's faeces, where it remains active. Typhus kills lice as well as people, but is vigorous for several weeks even in the tiny, decomposing corpse of the louse. Anybody who scratched an itch in an area inhabited by typhus-carrying lice was liable to contract the disease. In the 1890s human body lice thrived in crowded households. They were most easily killed by washing clothes and bedding in boiling – not merely hot, but boiling – water. Crofthouses in South Uist and Eriskay almost all contained large families in a small space, and rarely had boiling water in their washing tubs. Once the virus arrived it was difficult to extinguish, and there were no safe isolation wards in which to care for the victims.

The epidemic reached its peak in the spring and summer of 1897, when in a four-month period about 19 people died from typhus in South Uist and Eriskay and countless others were infected.* Fear and confusion stalked the islands. 'The people, panic-stricken,' wrote John Percival Day, 'fled from the infected and left them to the care of a few devoted men led by the doctor and the priest.' That this terrified survival impulse pertained throughout the islands is confirmed by the reference in Father Allan's poem 'Eilein na h-Oige' to 'Yon epidemic's selfishness' in Eriskay. All of the priests of the district performed their pastoral duties to the afflicted, but in Daliburgh Father George Rigg was at the centre of the storm. 'Day after day, for weeks past,' wrote a Lochboisdale correspondent to the *Oban Times* in August 1897, 'Father Rigg [was] attending cases of fever and nursing the patients from morning till night as no other person, not even the nearest relatives, would venture within a gun shot of the infected houses.'

Father George found himself at the end of July and beginning of August caring for a cottar's small family. The husband, the wife and their single child had all been infected. George Rigg 'unassisted nursed the sick household, cooking for them and performing all the necessary and unpleasant offices attaching to his self-imposed task.' He reportedly changed all his clothes before entering and after leaving the cottage. But on 4 August 1897, George Rigg caught typhus fever and was confined to bed at Allan MacDonald's old home in the priest's house at Daliburgh.

He died nine days later. He was 37 years old. George Rigg's coffin was carried across the machair from St Peter's Church to Hallin cemetery by six island priests, including Father James Chisholm of Barra, Father John Mackintosh of Bornish and Father Allan MacDonald of Eriskay. 'The procession... was rendered still more touching by the mournful strains of the different laments played on the bagpipes.'

---

* The exact number is impossible to confirm, as many deaths in the district at that time were not investigated or certified by qualified people before burial. In the ten years between 1891 and 1901, it has been deduced, 770 deaths in South Uist were uncertified by doctors.

The sacrificial death of George Rigg attracted national press coverage and tributes from all quarters. It seemed, as more than one reporter noted, to echo in an industrial age the saintly devotions of a much more innocent world. Father Allan mourned his 'truest friend' publicly and privately. He wrote in Gaelic a bardic elegy which recalled that when the news of the death reached Eriskay, 'I'll take long to forget / The cry of grief that was heard / With our minds like a world without sun'.

In the journal which he began to keep in the following month, Allan MacDonald reflected long and hard. He suffered an obvious human personal loss, about which he felt slightly guilty, not least because it was a selfish instinct and the manner of Father George's death epitomised selflessness. He wrote without complete conviction,

> The loss of the want of a thorough friend, who can thoroughly understand you and can sympathise with you and to whom you lay open your mind and views without reserve is a privation but not to us so great who live isolated as to many others, as we are bound to be trained by having the years of experience of being without a single near absolute friend to this state of negative privation.

But there was more.

> May his sincere holiness, and the clear perception of the duties and dignity of the priesthood that he had, teach me to think what I ought to be and to strive to be what I should be. His struggles against his strong self . . . his suspicions that self was really at the bottom of the physical prostrations that came over him . . . Poor Fr Rigg will yet be known and appreciated and the influence of his life and death will go to teach us to hate self and suspect self and to love our fellow man whoever he be as the brother of Christ . . .

Father Allan MacDonald was writing as much about himself as

about the late Father George Rigg. They had been close friends for better reasons than they knew. They shared more than their tall stature and their age. They were jointly and individually involved in an intellectual effort to define the nature and purpose of their vocation. It was an introspection from which few Catholic priests may be immune.

Shortly after the death of Father George Rigg, Allan Mac-Donald re-adopted the precepts of the Apostolic Union of Priests. He had engaged at some point earlier in his life with that programme. 'One year only I look back to with less regret than to any other,' he wrote, 'a year in which I lived by the Rules of the Society of Priests called the Apostolic Union.' In 1897 he needed once again to discover a vocational lifestyle which might calm his doubts and justify himself to himself.

The Apostolic Union of Secular Priests* had been inspired by a Bavarian clergyman in the seventeenth century. Its function in the late nineteenth and early twentieth centuries was partly to ease, through 'a uniform rule of life', the crippling loneliness which was often felt by priests, such as Father Allan MacDonald, 'who are scattered far apart'. In such a brotherhood, it was hoped, 'The dangers of solitude are removed, and there is a concentrated effort on the part of all to attain the common end. Each priest under these conditions devotes himself to the well-being and perfection of all, and, though prevented by the cares of his ministry from

---

* 'In the language of religious the world (sæculum) is opposed to the cloister; religious who follow a rule, especially those who have been ordained, form the regular clergy, while those who live in the world are called the secular clergy ... The secular cleric makes no profession and follows no religious rule, he possesses his own property like laymen, he owes to his bishop canonical obedience, not the renunciation of his own will, which results from the religious vow of obedience; only the practice of celibacy in Holy Orders is identical with the vow of chastity of the religious. The secular clergy, in which the hierarchy essentially resides, always takes precedence of the regular clergy of equal rank ...' – The Catholic Encyclopaedia

enjoying the advantages of living in community, he does not feel that he is deprived of the benefits of the religious family; nor are the counsels and assistance of his brothers wanting.'

Parts of the function of the Apostolic Union could have been tailored bespoke for Father Allan in Eriskay. He wrote that, 'without one absolutely thorough near friend in whom I can confide trouble and with whom I can interchange views to say nothing of the *solatium humanum* [human solace] which the enjoyment of such friendship throws over one's life, it is no wonder I feel solitary, and find myself to a certain extent left painfully alone and poised somewhere in vacuity.'

The code of the Apostolic Union offered Father Allan and his fellows 'the spiritual exercises and the ecclesiastical study for each day, each week, each month, each year, and counsels with regard to the holy ministry'. They became members of a fraternity of the mind.

The Apostolic Union's four pastoral priorities were not only attractive to Father Allan; they were perfectly suited to the work of a nineteenth-century Hebridean priest.

> Preaching was to bring out the infinite amiability of Christ and preachers were to set themselves to instruct their hearers. Catechetics: the greatest energy was to be given to the instruction of children and the ignorant and priests were to adapt their teaching to the capacity of the classes. Sacrament of Penance: priests were to display the charity of Christ and were not only to hear confessions but were to direct. The sick, poor, and afflicted: the priests of the Union were to have a special regard for these groups.

The Union also gave him a timetable, which he would follow in Eriskay to the best of his ability, in the reassuring knowledge that from Britain to Bavaria hundreds of other clergymen were doing the same. He was to rise at a fixed hour – around 5.00 a.m. – each day after seven hours of sleep. He would pray for half an hour before Mass. He would then read the Bible for 30 minutes. He would study theology and read the Life of Christ each day. He would be in bed before 10.00 p.m. each night.

The last, and even the first, cannot have been easily observed in Eriskay on ceilidh nights. And Father Allan certainly broke some other directives which forbade playing cards, taking journeys simply to satisfy a curiosity and being alone with members of the opposite sex, if only because collecting folklore could be described as a 'curiosity' and he lived alone with a housekeeper called Kate. A man who subscribed to a number of publications, including the *Oban Times*, the *London Weekly Times* and until it folded in the early 1880s, that radical voice of the region *The Highlander*, would not comfortably have heard the warning that 'The Associates are to keep themselves on their guard against the flood of newspapers and of empty pamphlets from which there is nothing, or next to nothing, to be gained'.

But Father Allan sought discipline and structure in his 'useless, sinful, ungrateful life'. In the words of Father Michael MacDonald, 'He struggles to keep the programme laid down by the Apostolic Union and amazes himself when he manages to keep it even indifferently for a few weeks'.

During his first four years in Eriskay Allan MacDonald improved and collated his folklore collection. He complained in December 1897 that he was 'without material to add to the folklore notes (having practically exhausted my immediate neighbourhood), without the ability of walking whither I may get more . . .' But by early 1898 he had filled six quarto notebooks with his small, neat handwriting, and four of them had been written in Eriskay. It was, said John Lorne Campbell after editing Father Allan MacDonald's separate anthology of 'Gaelic words and expressions from South Uist and Eriskay' in 1953, 'one of the largest and most valuable collections of general folklore associated with one particular district that has ever been brought together in Scotland'.

He knew that he was recording the cultural expressions of a civilisation which was in decline. He recognised that the slow but inexorable fall in the numbers of monoglot Gaelic speakers reduced the depth and quality of the language. He realised, as did most of his late nineteenth-century colleagues in the field, that he was leaving traces for posterity. He knew better than some of his colleagues that the homage which was implicit in taking respectful note of his parishioners' language and customs made a small contribution to restoring the self-esteem of a vulnerable people.

But he also collected Gaelic lore and lexicography simply because they enthralled him. However much he rebuked himself for his supposedly irreverent and selfish hobby, he could not stop. He adored and duly transcribed the great fables, epic traditional tales and songs. But everything in the vicinity intrigued him, from the news that during the failure of the potato crop Hebridean Gaels ate gooseweed instead, to the important calculation that it took '13 carts of decayed seaweed [used as manure] to raise 1 barrel of potatoes, and 4 fresh seaweed to make 1 decayed.' He noted – and shared enthusiastically with visitors – that the root of sneezewort could be smoked instead of tobacco, that the root of tormentil was used for tanning and that each family killed a sheep for Christmas. His care for such details as much as for Ossianic lays distinguished him and helps to explain the respect in which he would be held by twentieth- and twenty-first-century scholars.

Allan MacDonald had a Gaelic learner's fascination with minutiae. Teaching himself the language almost from scratch, he had noted and memorised its huge and colourful lexicon word by word. Unique phrases and expressions which a native of South Uist and Eriskay – or even a native fluent Gaelic speaker from elsewhere – would have taken for granted and not considered worthy of special attention, lodged themselves in his mind.

Introducing Allan MacDonald's anthology of words and phrases, John Lorne Campbell wrote,

It supplements and completes, on the lexicographical side, the important researches on the dialects of South Uist and Barra of Professor Carl Hj. Borgstrøm of Oslo; it contains literally scores of words which were falling out of use during Fr. Allan's time, and which are not to be found in other dictionaries; it explains many difficult passages in Gaelic folktales and folksongs.

Every aspect of Hebridean life is illustrated by this Collection. From it can be obtained an idea of the vivid, concrete and epigrammatical speech of nineteenth-century Hebridean Gaelic-speakers, of their customs, habits and work, of their strong religious sense and their keen observation of the animals and plants around them; from it can be gained an insight into the wealth of folklore and oral tradition which the Gaels preserved in spite of poverty, oppression and the official persecution of their language, the tradition which lay behind their thoughts and provided so many allusions in their everyday conversation ...

The MS of the Collection, which is arranged under initial letters but is not in alphabetical order, was begun in 1893, the year Fr Allan went to Eriskay, and was nearing completion in November 1897. The initial date is apparent from the fact that the first entries under nearly every letter are taken from a collection of waulking songs made by the late Donald MacCormick of Kilpheder in South Uist in 1893; the latter date is proved by the fact that another notebook shows that the last entry under letter M, 'mùdag' ... was taken down from Christina MacInnes on Eriskay on 27 November, 1897.

The basis of the Collection is the oral tradition of Uist and Eriskay (whose inhabitants originally came, around 1850, from the Beinn Mhór district of South Uist and various islands in Barra Sound) with allusions to Benbecula, Barra, and Mingulay. Some of the story-tellers and folksingers who were Fr Allan's informants were monoglot Gaelic speakers born before the battle of Waterloo. It would be impossible to make a comparable collection of words to-day.

Fr Allan's method was to note down the words and phrases which he heard which were not to be found in the Gaelic Dictionary of Fr Ewen MacEachen (1842), or which varied from the forms given by Fr MacEachen, who based his Dictionary on the dialect of Arisaig. Fr Allan also noted such words from the poems of Allan MacDougall (Ailean Dall), Alexander MacDonald, John MacCodrum, Rob Donn, the Rev. Angus MacDonald (parish priest of Barra 1805–25), and Donald Campbell. He notes nearly a hundred words from the poems of Ailean Dall, who was connected with his own native district ...

The Collection reveals, then, the nature of the Gaelic library possessed by Fr Allan McDonald. It included the first editions of the dictionaries of Fr MacEachen and Alexander MacBain, Duncan Campbell's Gaelic Songs (1798), the Stewarts' Collection of Gaelic Songs (1804), the second edition of Allan MacDougall's poems (1829) (there has been no edition since, and this is now a very rare book), the 1874 edition of Alexander MacDonald's poems, an edition of 'Sàr Obair nam Bàrd Gàidhealach', and an early edition of the Fate of the Children of Lir, published by the Society for the Preservation of the Irish Language. He also had Donald MacCormick's MS collection of waulking songs referred to, and his own MS collections.

All the words collected by Fr Allan are given with a wealth of illustrative phrases, folklore and anecdote, which make his Collection more readable, perhaps, than any other dictionary.

It would have been a formidable lifetime's achievement by a full-time collector. The busy priest Allan MacDonald had made it in less than ten years.* His work as a folklorist alone would have cemented his reputation.

---

* Allan MacDonald would self-disparagingly and misleadingly tell a visitor that he had been unable to collect much material while he was in South Uist – 'I had no time then to go to waulkings!' But: 'Then came his break-down, and thereafter for a while no work at all. Then Eriskay; where, in what he called his leisure, he could busy himself at the setting-down of sgeulan, Ossianic lays, rannan, words of songs, idioms, old-words, and all such ...'

In his own time it attracted virtually every specialist in the field to his door. In 1895 a Cornishman, Celtic language specialist and keeper of manuscripts at the British Museum visited him in Eriskay. Henry Jenner, a self-confessed latter-day Jacobite from the English west country, was in search of the footsteps of Prince Charles Edward Stuart. He found instead an incomparable host, 'A king in his own island . . . nor was there anyone in all the Isles like him for folk-lore.'

As we have seen, Father Allan refused to hoard or claim any personal copyright of the material. That abnegation of the 'strong self', the 'suspect self', baffled and annoyed some of his secular friends and admirers. The odd case of Ada Goodrich-Freer was the main source of their irritation.

Ada Goodrich-Freer was a charming fantasist and borderline fraud. Allan MacDonald responded to her charm, tolerated her fantasies and knew nothing of anything worse. Goodrich-Freer's skein of deceptions was expertly unravelled by Trevor Hall and John Lorne Campbell for their 1968 book *Strange Things*. Among other curiosities, Hall and Campbell discovered, she was born of ordinary English stock in Rutland as plain Ada Freer. She died in the United States claiming Scottish descent and a privileged county background as Adela Monica Goodrich-Freer Spoer, three-fifths of that name being strictly accurate. When she was about 36, Ada Goodrich-Freer knocked 13 years off her age and became 23 years old again. She never restored the missing years. She was an extremely pretty blonde.

Ada Goodrich-Freer travelled to South Uist in 1894 on behalf of the Society for Psychical Research, subsidised by no less a sponsor than the Marquess of Bute, to investigate the Celtic phenomenon of second sight. She was linguistically and culturally unqualified to research anything in the Scottish Gaidhealtachd. In 1894 she was in her thirty-eighth year but the gentlemen of the Society, whose psychical powers were clearly confounded by attractive blondes, thought her to be a precociously gifted 24 year-old. She was directed to Father Allan MacDonald by the Reverend Peter Dewar, a Church of Scotland minister from Bute who was the secretary in Scotland of the Society for Psychical Research. Reverend Dewar had in his turn been alerted to Father Allan's knowledge of Gaelic traditions by William MacKenzie of the Crofters Commission.

Early in August 1894 Ada Goodrich-Freer wrote to the Marquess of Bute from the priest's house in Eriskay:

> The Rev Allan Macdonald, under whose hospitable roof I have been staying... I find to be a cultured, devout and charming person. He has lived all his life in the Highlands – and deeply loves the Highlanders; their beliefs – their traditions – their songs and their lore. He seems to me to be a thorough master of the Gaelic Language, and has been so good as to present me with a collection of Gaelic Hymns which he edited and published a few years ago. Several of the hymns in this collection are his own composition and seem to me to be very beautiful.

Allan MacDonald gave more than his Gaelic hymnal to Ada Goodrich-Freer. As was his habit, he instantly shared all of his collection. Although she was in no way able to assess or to edit the collection, she recognised its value to herself. She flattered and encouraged his efforts. She persuaded him to gather and send to her local stories about second sight. She also copied and took away with her large amounts of Father Allan's researches which had nothing to do with second sight. She arranged for the Marquess of Bute's secretary to send this 'very poor priest' a cheque for £10 in compensation. After that she proceeded to regard Father Allan's collection as her own resource.

Ada Goodrich-Freer returned to the southern Outer Hebrides in 1896 and 1898. By the latter date she had, on the mainland of England and Scotland, presented papers and published essays on subjects as diverse as 'The Norsemen in the Hebrides' and 'Christian Legends of the Hebrides'. They drew heavily upon Father Allan's manuscripts but if he was acknowledged at all it was as one source among others, rather than as the main seam of the material which she was assiduously mining.

When Ada Goodrich-Freer arrived for the last time in Eriskay in August 1898, Father Allan already had company. He was entertaining Walter Blaikie and Everard Feilding. Feilding, an English barrister, was a member of the Society for Psychical Research, so it is likely that he expected to meet Goodrich-Freer there.

Walter Biggar Blaikie was a different matter altogether. Blaikie was the son of an eminent Scottish Presbyterian divine called William Garden Blaikie. William Garden Blaikie was a founding member of the Free Church of Scotland, a writer, a social reformer and a temperance campaigner. His son Walter trained and worked as a civil engineer before entering the printing and publishing business in Edinburgh. By 1898 he was 50 years old, an accomplished amateur photographer and a Highland historian and writer who published through the Scottish History Society books on the 'Itinerary of Prince Charles Edward' and the 'Origins of the '45'.

Walter Blaikie was also a director of T & A Constable Ltd, the Edinburgh publishing house which was, at the end of the nineteenth century, preparing to issue the fruits of Alexander Carmichael's decades of collecting 'words, rites, and customs, dying and obsolete' in the Scottish Gaidhealtachd. The combination of those interests, as well as the priest's growing celebrity, drew Walter Blaikie to Father Allan MacDonald.

It was a curious summer house party in Eriskay in 1898. Walter Blaikie busied about taking excellent staged photographs of everyday Eriskay life and people. Ada Goodrich-Freer quizzed Father Allan further on second sight and other Hebridean survivals. ('The songs and the sgeulachdan [stories] were all driven over here from [the mainland],' he would tell visitors. 'They could get no further, and here they have stayed.')

It was an enjoyable but futile exercise. They were on separate tracks. Allan MacDonald understood second sight as part of the complex belief system of the Highlands and Islands, and as a source of popular legend and mythology rather than an everyday method of practical divination. Goodrich-Freer was looking for irrefutable evidence of psychical activity. He knew that foresights, fears, suspicions, coincidences, inexplicable visions and unanswered prayers, accumulated over many centuries, still informed the credence of many late-nineteenth-century Gaels, including such hard-headed men of the world as the South Uist School Board's attendance officer, Donald MacCormick. He also understood that there are more things in heaven and earth than are dreamt of in human philosophy. She wanted the supernatural equivalent of an accurate weather forecast.*

At one point Blaikie arranged for a group photograph to be taken, possibly by Everard Feilding, of Blaikie himself, Ada Goodrich-Freer, her companion Miss Constance Moore and Father Allan MacDonald.

It made a marvellous vignette. Walter Blaikie knelt on the turf at the right of the group, gazing deeply at the lens from behind an impressive white moustache. By his left arm sat Constance Moore holding a pale terrier whose name was Scamp. Slightly in front of Miss Moore, Ada Goodrich-Freer, looking all of her 41 years, averted her eyes from the camera and peered pensively at the ground. Both ladies wore dark capes and tam o' shanter bonnets. To their left, slightly apart from the group, sat Father Allan. He wore polished leather gaiters over his boots, a casual jacket, his clerical collar and a battered, wide-brimmed hat. He too looked

---

* 'I wonder what they *really are*,' Father Allan MacDonald's Eriskay housekeeper was reported as musing after telling a visitor about water-horses in 1905. 'Is it just *creatures*? – or is it – *you* know!' 'Did you ever see one?' asked the visitor. 'No – not I! *But plenty I know that has.*'

straight at the camera. Approaching his fortieth year, he had lost the bulkiness of his youth. He had the face of a rare species: a kindly intellectual. He was thin. His eyes were wryly amused and the corners of his mouth twitched in the hint of a smile, as if to ask of the cameraman, or his company of associates, or of life in general: what a strange performance is this?

That gathering marked the end of one friendship and the beginning of another. Although they corresponded, Ada Goodrich-Freer never saw Father Allan or the Hebrides again. Her research into Highland second sight was largely dismissed by the Society for Psychical Research, and her career and reputation there fell apart. As it collapsed, so did her elaborately contrived image. In 1901 Alexander Carmichael wrote to tell Allan MacDonald that 'Miss Freer is not altogether what she seems' and, 'We hear from various sources that Ms Freer is not genuine and some call her a clever imposter. I never got my wife to believe in her.'

Carmichael thought that he was gently disillusioning his friend, a good but naïve person in a remote place, of a woman for whom Father Allan had felt affection. It may not have occurred to him that Father Allan could have suspected Ada Goodrich-Freer's frailties for several years, and simply had not minded them very much.

In 1903 Miss Goodrich-Freer published *Outer Isles*, a 450-page book about the Hebrides which was suffused with local lore. She credited the work of Allan MacDonald and Alexander Carmichael (they had twenty and seven references in the index respectively), without paying them the full homage that many considered to be their due. *Outer Isles* was dedicated to 'Connie' Moore and Scamp the dog. She then went to live in Jerusalem, where she met and married a German-American called Hans Henry Spoer. The Spoers moved to the United States in 1923 and Adela Monica Goodrich-Freer Spoer died there eight years later. The bereaved Hans Henry apparently thought her to be only 56. She was 73 years old and had, in the words of Trevor Hall, 'enjoyed a long and eventful life'.

She left an account of Father Allan in *Outer Isles* which would once again have caused his mouth to twitch and his eyes to crinkle with amusement.

His life is one from which most educated men would shrink as from a slow martyrdom, a living death. He has now happily a neat and comfortable house overlooking the Minch toward the island of South Uist. It is enclosed, and by blasting some of the rocks a fair piece of ground, perhaps some quarter of an acre, has been made available for cultivation and for the care of ducks and poultry.

There is a tiny oratory [in the priest's house] where there is daily Mass, seldom unattended, and this little centre of 'Sweetness and Light' is visible from almost every part of the island. But when one thinks of the utter loneliness of such a life, of the distance from any person who can even speak the English language, none probably, in any degree companionable nearer than Dalibrog, when one remembers the dangerous Minch dividing the islet from even such amenities as are furnished by South Uist, and the fierce waves of the Atlantic beating it on every side, it seems as if even the lives of the hermits of old were not more sacrificial, more heroic, than this!

Walter Blaikie composed a slightly less dramatic tribute to his visit. He wrote to Eriskay from Edinburgh in September 1898,

If I live to be a hundred, I shall never forget those happy days spent with you and our happy party. I am already longing to go back to you and am looking forward to next spring when it will be possible to go if other things permit. I learned so much and saw so much when with you that my mind is still too full to assimilate it all and it will take me some time to arrange in my mind the matter that I learned and noted when with you. From my heart I thank you, my dear Father, for all your intense kindness and priceless hospitality.

Blaikie did return the following year, took more photographs and absorbed more of the Hebridean life. In 1900 his company, T & A Constable, published 300 copies of the first volume of Alexander Carmichael's magnum opus, *Carmina Gadelica, Ortha nan Gaidheal** – *Hymns and Incantations with Illustrative Notes on Words, Rites, and Customs, Dying and Obsolete: Orally Collected in the Highlands and Islands of Scotland and Translated into English*. It finally established Carmichael as the doyen of *fin de siècle* folklorists.

Alexander Carmichael was born in the Argyllshire island of Lismore in 1832. He worked for all of his life as an exciseman in the Highlands and Islands, 'from Arran to Caithness, from Perth to St Kilda'. While on his professional journeys, by boat and packhorse and on foot, lodging, travelling and meeting with all the people of the north and west of Scotland, in the 1850s he began to collect their hymns, stories, songs, curses and incantations. He was struck time and again by the probable antiquity of what he heard from the mouths of his contemporary Gaels:

> It is the product of far-away thinking, come down on the long stream of time. Who the thinkers and whence the stream, who can tell? Some of the hymns may have been composed within the cloistered cells of Derry and Iona, and some of the incantations among the cromlechs of Stonehenge and the standing-stones of Callarnis. These poems were composed by the learned, but they have not come down through the learned, but through the unlearned – not through the lettered few, but through the unlettered many – through the crofters and cottars, the herdsmen and shepherds, of the Highlands and Islands.

Carmichael amassed material for almost half a century before the late 1890s and early 1900s, when he prepared his first two volumes

---

* The title is bilingual. The two phrases mean 'songs, hymns or incantations of the Gaels' in Latin and in Gaelic.

for publication. He died in 1912 and a further four volumes were published posthumously.

Like everybody else in the field of Gaelic lore, Carmichael visited South Uist regularly. 'These compositions,' he wrote in his introduction to *Carmina Gadelica*, 'have been rescued chiefly among Roman Catholics and in the islands.' He came to know and like Allan MacDonald as a fellow collector and as a man. Father Allan's collection was of course made readily available to Carmichael. But the first volume contained nothing from the priest's house in Eriskay – Carmichael had already amassed vast quantities of his own research, and he considered that Allan MacDonald's collection deserved, and would duly get, publication in its own right. 'The Rev. Father Allan Macdonald, Erisgey, South Uist,' explained Carmichael, 'generously placed at my disposal a collection of religious folk-lore made by himself. For this I am very grateful, though unable to use the manuscript, having so much material of my own.' That Carmichael should credit in print a man whose contributions he had been unable to use was a unique indication of the author's regard for Allan MacDonald.

Walter Blaikie was also convinced by 1899 that Father Allan MacDonald's collection merited a book of its own. 'You have given so much help to others,' he wrote to his new friend, 'and your own name as author should be known now. I shall not give you rest about this but shall press you on with it.'

Blaikie was as good as his word. He did continue to press Allan MacDonald to publish his manuscripts. Father Allan never did so. But four years later the two men would discover a reward for the collection which was more congenial to the priest than seeing his 'own name as author'.

Other authors were however growing used to painting Father Allan's character, both under his own real name in non-fiction and with a fictional name in novels. The tall, handsome man with a ready wit and impressive intellect who devoted himself to the poor on the margins of Europe became a magnet to writers. The phenomenon had begun in the early 1890s, when a young man named Frederic Breton visited South Uist.

Breton was born in Paddington in 1865. He was the son of a London solicitor who happened to be a Roman Catholic, and who therefore sent the young Frederic to be educated by monks at Fort Augustus Abbey School in the Scottish Highlands. Frederic later returned to London and entered journalism as a copyeditor. Like many journalists, he nursed the ambition to become an author of books. During his schooldays the neighbourhood of Fort Augustus, outside the abbey, had been largely a Gaelic-speaking district. This acquaintanceship with the culture and some secondhand knowledge of the traditional Catholic islands in the far west led Frederic Breton to travel north again in his mid 20s. He met Father Allan MacDonald in Daliburgh. Breton was given the usual visitor's unfettered access to Father Allan's researches into South Uist's history and traditions. He returned to London and in 1893, at the age of 28, he published a two-volume novel called *Heroine in Homespun*. It was set in South Uist, it was garishly coloured with Hebridean legend and it featured a charismatic young priest called Father MacCrimmon. *Heroine in Homespun* sank, leaving very little trace. Frederic Breton sensibly turned to writing non-fiction.

Father Allan's second representation in fiction was more successful. Its author, Neil Munro, was four years younger than Allan MacDonald. Munro had been born in the Argyllshire village of Inveraray to a single mother in 1863. Ann Munro was 33 and a kitchenmaid at the time. She raised Neil with the help of her mother. Both women were Celts to their roots and Neil was given Gaelic as his first language. He would make his fortune and reputation in written English, but he never lost his mother's tongue.

By 1901 Neil Munro had moved to Glasgow and become an acclaimed journalist and novelist. That summer, following the successful publication of *Doom Castle*, he set off for the Outer Hebrides in search of subject matter for another book. He sailed in August from Oban to Barra in the company of a friend who was a schools inspector with duties to perform in the Hebrides. They met Father James Chisholm in Barra, and a fishing skiff then took Neil Munro and the inspector of schools from Northbay across the sound to Eriskay. He later remembered,

> Till that time I had never heard the name of Father Allan MacDonald, nor even knew that there was a priest on the island to which we sailed. Under a thwart of the boat there was a box, and in idle curiosity I asked one of the boatmen what was in it.
>
> 'M'anam fhein cha'n'eil fhios agam,' he protested, ''s e rudeigenn a fhuair sinn 'n raoir air son Maighstir Ailean.'*

Neil Munro then found himself on an island 'enjoying the privileges of British citizenship, but in the most meagre form; virtually without roads, steamer connection, or telegraph, Eriskay did not learn of the death of Queen Victoria till nine days after the event [seven months earlier].'

Munro and the inspector went first to Eriskay School,

> ... and the inspection of its bright and healthy-looking children had scarcely started when a stranger entered. A man over six feet, lean, and greatly younger-looking than his age, which at the time was about forty, wearing a tweed suit and cap, and with no hint of his profession beyond the clerical collar – the first impression we got of Father Allan was of a personality curiously unpriestlike in its boyish cheerfulness, as well as in externals.
>
> He insisted that we should come to lunch at the Presbytery House – his dwelling on an eminence above the school. It was a Friday; we lunched on sea-trout, and there was a bottle of some unfamiliar Spanish wine.

---

* 'On my soul, I don't know. It is something we got last night for Father Allan.'

It was there our boatman's tact revealed itself; for on our mentioning that it was the first fish we had seen in the Outer Islands, Father Allan said, 'Well, I'm lucky to have them. The truth is that these good boatmen from North Bay heard last night you were coming here today, and knowing I was likely to be ill-provided for visitors on a Friday, they took these trout over with them in a box. I hope the remote possibility that they may have been poached will not impair their flavour . . .!'

It did not take long to discover that in this gentle, kindly priest there were many rare and shining qualities. He delighted in his people, he had a passion for his isle, and yet his mind ranged far beyond his office and the limits of his parish . . .

It was less of himself and his work that Father Allan talked than of things he thought more likely to interest the strangers. He proved – as more than one student of folk-lore and history has discovered with profit – an inexhaustible mine of information regarding the ancient Highland customs and beliefs that linger yet in Eriskay, the best of them encouraged eagerly by himself.

The results of his research in these directions, as we know, were free to all competent to consider them; and yet it is probable that a great mass of matter accumulated by him has never yet been published; at least he wrote me later of a considerable collection of notes untouched.

That summer day, under the guidance of its priest, we saw Eriskay at its best. It was not ill to share, there and then, his half-beliefs in *daoine sith* [fairy people] and second sight, to think that all the gods have not yet flown from high Olympus. I was wearing a suit of *crotal* dye, the tincture made from lichen. Laughingly he professed astonishment that I had found boatmen in Barra willing to ferry me in such a garb, for Barra believes that the *crotal* ever hankers for its native rock, and who so wears it in a boat courts sure destruction.

After their lunch of poached sea-trout, Allan MacDonald and Neil Munro walked around Eriskay.

His folk came about him unabashed and affectionately, it was to us a little strange to find them on such a footing with him of free speech, and even raillery, the raillery that intuitively knows the proper bounds, and is based on esteem and fondness. And at last he saw us to our boat on the shore.

On these sands, he said, the people, young and old, knelt in prayer when all that was mortal of each departed islander set out on its final voyage to the burial ground in Uist.

The fact aroused, and still arouses, a great and moving mental picture, but I cherish another – of the lonely figure of Father Allan waving his farewell on the sands at Rudha Chlaidh, and walking slowly, with bent head, upward to his dwelling, and turning again in the wind, and the cry of the uncomforted sea, and waving one last time as our sails filled and we passed from the isle of his dreams and his devotion into the tumult of the Sound, and into the wise world of towns and cities and men.

Neil Munro was a level-headed, even sceptical man who did not hesitate to shred undeserved reputations. But ever afterwards, he wrote, the white sands, clustered cottages and bare hills of Eriskay would be 'the background to my mental picture of a singularly lovable and disinterested and devoted soul. And he loved this pathetic little island – all its not unpleasing barrenness, its people and their ancient ways.'

The two men corresponded but never met again. Thereafter, to Munro 'the Outer Isles, so far as I was concerned, had their centre in the little island of Eriskay ... the archetype of all that is best and most interesting among the good and interesting people [of the Hebrides].'

Father Allan MacDonald, a son of Lochaber, spent as much time ministering in Oban and South Uist as he did in Eriskay. But Neil Munro – and Ada Goodrich-Freer and many others – identified a connection between the man and the 'pathetic little island' which was impossible to break. For much of the twentieth century Eriskay and Father Allan became synonymous. Their characters fitted like tongue and groove. They were orphaned émigrés, stoically making the best of their adopted rock in the North Atlantic Ocean. Those visitors such as Goodrich-Freer, who saw medieval eremitism in Father Allan's life on that rock, got both the island and its pastor wrong. Like his fellow members of the Apostolic Union, he was a secular clergyman. He lived in the world, among people – among 450 people in Eriskay. They were all, including their priest, ascetics by necessity who made humour and joy and culture and courtesy in their unpromising circumstances. He delighted in visitors and in corresponding with like minds from 'the wise world of towns and cities'. He visited the mainland perhaps once a year. But he could never have lived in that world. Eriskay gave him the base and the extended family from which he could reach out with confidence. It stabilised his mental and physical health. His love of the island was composed partly of gratitude. Eriskay, which was not used to gratitude, let alone love, from any quarter, responded in kind.

The urban dweller Neil Munro wrestled with the apparent contradiction of one of the finest intellects of his generation choosing to confine itself in one of the smallest and most isolated inhabited islands in Europe.

Many times, on stormy nights, in distant towns and cities, I thought of him out there, 'far amid the melancholy main', a sovereign in his tiny kingdom, standing at his doorway in the sound of the surf and in the darkness, all the world obliterated except for the lights in the crofts below, and tried to imagine his thoughts in such an hour and situation.

Was he lonely there, who had seen life in its busiest eddies? Among the drifting sands and disconsolate rains, did he pine for sunshine and flowers who had lived bland summers in Old Castile? Was he ever a prey to that discontent that comes on men in a constant environment intellectually lower than themselves?

To a calculating and worldly mind he might seem a man 'lost', as the saying goes, in that remote and narrow corner of the Roman Catholic world, but gentleness and devotion and self-effacement are never thrown away, and serve God's purpose anywhere.

Munro failed to square the circle. Gentleness and devotion certainly served Father Allan's vocation as well in Eriskay as anywhere. But he did not regard his fellow islanders as being in any sense 'lower' than himself. In many respects he recognised and deferred to their superiority. He wished both to serve and learn from them.

Two years after his visit to Eriskay, Neil Munro published a novel titled *Children of Tempest*. It was set in South Uist, Barra and Mingulay. It featured an astute and popular priest in the Uist parish of Boisdale called Father Ludovick. 'He was a man about thirty-five years old, tall and spare, beloved of his folk, who called him faithfully behind his back "Lord of the Isles", half for his mother's name that had been Macdonald, half for his attributes of lovable wise command. A king in some respects, and yet a child in his simplicities.'

Father Ludovick enjoyed Iberian wine and daydreamed occasionally of Spain: 'Valladolid and the guitar – Heaven help me! – and morning in a wayside wine-shop at breakfast...' The fictional priest told another of Munro's characters,

How glad we should be to have escaped the world with all its distractions, and find peace here and the simple way ... [I can walk] when I will, uplifted on the mists of Hecla and Benmore. I own the Isles from Barra Head to the very Butt of Lewis so far as I can ride or sail a skiff; the sea is mine to the dip of it and all the winds come neighbourly to my door; would I change for a display of stone and mortar, and a bottle, the mood that makes me free of all, and one and equal with the universe?

Allan MacDonald's own creative literary life flowered in Eriskay.

He continued with increasing confidence and ability to write the Gaelic verses with which he had experimented at Valladolid. He wrote secular and devotional poems, hymns and songs of an increasingly high standard.

He struggled constantly with ways of communicating the faith to his remote and insular congregation. 'The recital of St Adamnan's "Vision",' he wrote, 'was a lesson . . . more effective than a hundred sermons. Could I devise a Tale of the kind that would fix even one useful idea indelibly on their minds. I might compose one such, but I doubt if I could make it interesting or classical enough to take with them.'

He never ceased to feel that his adopted Gaelic was inadequate. The Eriskay people might insist that there was 'Gaidhlig gu leoir aig Maighstir Ailein' – plenty of Gaelic in Father Allan – but he knew that the compliment was relative. When he had written a short play in the language, he ruefully said that any one of the islanders acting in his drama 'could put better words into it than these'. (A modest comment which was promptly illustrated when an Eriskay man, rehearsing his part, improved some of his lines.)

'I never write a thing that pleases me,' he said, 'but I find it better said already in some [other composer's] song.'

But Allan MacDonald was literate, imaginative and devoted to Gaelic. He wrote hymns for his congregation which would still be sung in the Catholic Hebrides in the twenty-first century. He wrote reflective verses on the beauty of his environment. He wrote Gaelic poetry of a millennial quality which would be reflected even in English translation. He wrote of the winter weather that enfolded Eriskay like a sleeping woman, 'Till warmth releases her breath', and of the perfect daisies which then decorated the meadows, 'Gold is your heart, snow is your lip, / Emerald is the stalk . . .'

Ged a dh'fheannadh reothadh earraich
Air an anmoch le chuid rann

H-uile h-ainmhidh am bheil anail
'S brat de ghlainidh air a' ghleann,
Fhads tha 'n t-adhar gun bhith salach,
Neoil ruith thairis 'nan deann,
S glaine lainnir suil na h-ainnir
Tha gar n-amharc far nam beann.

(Though at evening with its knife-blades
Springtime frost might flay
Every creature that's drawing breath
And in glass the glen's encased,
As long as the sky is free of rain,
And clouds are scurrying by,
There looks down at us from the mountains
The pure sparkle of the maiden's eye.)

He wrote serious elegies and joyful celebrations. He assumed in some ways the part of a traditional Celtic clan bard, recording the events of his community: its deaths and departures, unions and arrivals.

In that role Allan MacDonald wrote in February 1899 a long rhyming lyric which he read at the wedding party of his housekeeper Kate Campbell to an Eriskay fisherman called Donald Campbell. The whole piece exuded familiar hilarity. He made several witty references to the old hostilities between Clan Campbell and Clan Donald before conceding that 'it's not impossible that this pair / Are not quite as awful as other Campbells'. He poked fun at island priests. He paid tribute to the 'lovely sophisticated girls' of Eriskay, the grace of whose dancing would, he said, make fairy women envious.

That wedding ceremony would have taken place on a Tuesday evening, as was the tradition in Eriskay. By Wednesday morning he had lost his housekeeper. Kate was replaced by two other Campbell sisters. Mary and Penelope Campbell were the daughters of a fisherman and his wife from Bunavullin on the north coast of Eriskay. In 1899 they were 22 and 25 years old respectively. Mary married another Eriskay fisherman in 1906; her older sister Penelope was still single when she died in Eriskay in 1956 at the age of 82.

Penelope Campbell was proud and possessive of her employer at the priest's house. She 'held herself high and her office too, she knitted and span for Father Allan, and had the knack to make delicious even the salt fish and potatoes that were the best and all he got to eat for half the year . . . she kept the chapel-house a pattern for neatness and cleanliness, and her master carefree, so far as she was able.'

She was as full of song and stories as any of her people, which – despite her fondness for giving a traditional air a modern, Edwardian lilt – pleased her priest enormously. She was bilingual, thoroughly fluent in English, but deeply attached to her own heritage. One evening when Allan MacDonald and a visitor were talking in the priest's house, the term 'Celtic gloom' – which had been popularised by some of the less dependable writers of the era to describe the supposedly submissive attitude of Scottish and Irish Gaels on the eve of their extinction – occurred in their conversation. Penelope Campbell looked up sharply from her knitting.

'What's that?' she said.

'It's something an Englishman's writing about us,' said Father Allan.

'*How* does he know?' said Penelope Campbell. She knitted a little more. '*What* does he know about us anyway?'

One Sunday morning Penelope Campbell was escorting a guest to Mass when they came across Father Allan in front of the church in the middle of a knot of men. One man with a long white beard asked the priest forcibly in Gaelic what would happen if they did not obey the estate factor's order to dip their sheep. 'You'll get dipped yourselves,' said Father Allan, 'and the big-beards first.'

There was a roar of laughter as he turned on his heel and strode into church. The guest, having understood barely a word, looked inquisitively at Penelope Campbell.

'He's very witty, you know,' said Penelope demurely.

The church before which that exchange took place was not the cramped and draughty old St Michael's chapel above the sands of Coilleag. Father Allan MacDonald had built its replacement.

Nineteenth-century Hebridean priests were accustomed to building new churches. Allan MacDonald had lived for ten years with Father Alexander Campbell, the man who built St Peter's in Daliburgh. Father Allan's college friend James Chisholm had built a small chapel in Mingulay, and in the late 1880s he oversaw the creation of Our Lady Star of the Sea Church above the main town of Castlebay on the south coast of Barra. It opened its doors for the first time on Christmas Eve 1888. James Chisholm invited Father Allan MacDonald to travel from South Uist and preach the sermon in Castlebay that day.

In 1889 a proud Father James wrote presciently of his achievement in Castlebay:

> The church is beautiful in design, and the workmanship is substantial enough to withstand the Hebridean gales for a century or two to come. The site is extremely well chosen, resting on the crest of a rugged and steep crag, overlooking the village of Castlebay, and the historic castle [Kisimul] of the warlike MacNeils. It will be a landmark for the daring fishermen of Barra, as they venture to and from their deep-sea excursions . . . the church even now, in its unfinished state, can fairly claim to be second to no edifice erected for divine worship from the Butt of Lewis to the wave-worn cliffs of Barrahead.

In 1901 Neil Munro saw and marvelled at Our Lady Star of the Sea in Castlebay. Munro, who had been raised a Protestant and had briefly attended an Argyllshire Free Church school, arrived during the Feast of the Assumption on 15 August. 'I never thought . . .' he wrote afterwards, 'to see Gaels kneel before an image of the Virgin Mary, fingering rosaries, but here they are, and it seems the most natural thing in the world.'

A few days later in Eriskay, in that summer of 1901, 'It was with paternal pleasure' that Father Allan MacDonald showed Neil Munro 'the site of the new church – then unbuilt, but with the stones in readiness, and the sand for it which the children of the island had carried from the beach in their play-hours.'

Compared to Eriskay, Castlebay and Daliburgh were large parishes with at least a bit of disposable income. Our Lady Star of the Sea had been constructed with the help of a bequest from an affluent Barra merchant, and after substantial fund-raising. It was built at a time when the Diocese of Argyll and the Isles was in its first full flush of youth, led by the zealous Bishop Angus MacDonald and patronised by the Marquess of Bute. The Castlebay church was professionally designed by a mainland architect and erected by the Oban contractors MacDougall & MacColl, as well as employing the same South Uist mason, Iain 'Clachair' Campbell, who was responsible for the Bute Hospital in Daliburgh.

Whatever would be built in Eriskay early in the twentieth century could not expect such favours. Bute was dead, Bishop Angus was away, and the diocese was almost bankrupt.

But it still had its people. The new St Michael's Church was built on a site adjacent to the priest's house at Rubha Ban, 'exposed to the four winds of heaven'. Father Allan wrote and distributed a pamphlet requesting subscriptions from sympathisers. He also raised money from his own efforts. In March 1902 he received a letter from Walter Blaikie which once again urged him to put his folklore collection into print. Blaikie wrote from Edinburgh,

I know that you have collected much, more probably than any man living. I know that many people have had the use of your matter, sometimes without suitable acknowledgement. Now I think this is the very opportunity for letting the world know your work, and that this may be the chance for producing a worthy work in your own name and with some remuneration for it.

Allan MacDonald promptly posted to Blaikie all seven volumes of his collection. Blaikie paid for but never published them.* The remuneration went towards the new St Michael's Church.

The building received two other substantial injections of capital. One came famously from the Eriskay fishermen, who all agreed to devote the proceeds from a night's fishing to the project. John Lorne Campbell reported that 'after fervent prayer [they] caught a record catch, worth nearly £200, no small sum in those times'. The exact amount made by the fishermen was substantial but remains unclear. John Lorne Campbell suggested that it comprised the donation of £180 which was recorded in the building fund accounts in January 1902.

His American visitor Amy Murray quoted Father Allan as telling her, 'I waited until they had been having pretty good luck for a while, then I said to them, "Why not give one night's catch to the Church?" They laughed a little, but at last they said they would. That night they had the biggest catch of the whole year, and they gave the Church every pennyworth of it.'

---

* The notebook containing Father Allan's dictionary of Gaelic words and expressions singular to South Uist and Eriskay was recovered and edited by John Lorne Campbell and published in 1953. The other six books of handwritten transcribed folklore went in three different directions. At least two of them were given, we may presume by Walter Blaikie, to Alexander Carmichael, and were later delivered as part of the Carmichael–Watson Collection to Edinburgh University Library. Two of them found their way via George Henderson to the Henderson Collection in Glasgow University Library. The other two – the middle two – have disappeared. The four surviving folklore notebooks are currently being transcribed and edited by Ronald Black, who wonders if 'the reason why vols III and IV are now missing is that they remained in Blaikie's charge at Constable & Co'.

A South Uist priest would write shortly afterwards, 'They let down their nets in honour of Our Blessed Lady and St Michael. I understand the whole amount contributed by them was £280.'

The differences hardly matter. They were people who lived on the edge of famine and whose children went shoeless for much of the year, and they gave to their new church in 1902 the equivalent in purchasing power a century later of at least £80,000.

Father Allan received a similar sum – about £200 – from a man who had never been near to Eriskay. Marc-André Raffalovich was a wealthy, naturalised British subject who hosted a fashionable salon first in London's Mayfair and later in Edinburgh. He had been born in Paris in 1864 into a family of Russian Jewish émigrés. In 1896 he was received into the Roman Catholic Church. He was a writer, a patron of such artists as Aubrey Beardsley, and a homosexual who devoted much of his adult life to attempting to reconcile his Catholicism with his *unisexualité*. In around 1901 Raffalovich heard of Father Allan's work in Eriskay from a good friend who was about to be ordained as a Catholic priest in Scotland. At least two donations subsequently made their way from Raffalovich to Eriskay, for £100 in 1901 and for a further £75 early in 1903.

Those were the contributions which bought the lime and the slates and the glass and other basic building materials. The rest was done by the congregation. They quarried the stone from the side of Beinn Sgrithinn, the highest hill on the island. They carried sand for cement from the beaches up to Rubha Ban. With certain topographical differences, St Michael's Church in Eriskay would have been raised in much the same fashion as St Brendan's Chapel at Craigston in Barra, which was built under Father William Macdonell 40 years earlier. A Barra witness would remember of the Craigston church,

All the able-bodied Catholics in the island worked and laboured in one way or another at the building, even small boys did their bit. The boys brought cockle shells from Traigh Mhor in creels or baskets on the backs of the Barra ponies. These shells were burned into lime.

A smack with lime and slates landed a cargo at Castlebay. This cargo was conveyed to Craigston in the same manner. All the heavy wood used for couples and joists was drift wood washed ashore from the Atlantic ... [The materials] were conveyed to the building by Father Macdonell's cart and another belonging to a merchant in Castlebay, for the Crofters of Barra had no carts at this time. Father Macdonell collected as much money as he could amongst his Congregation; but this, I believe, did not amount to very much, as money was scarce here in those days. Father Macdonell also collected money in Glasgow and elsewhere. I am told that the cost of the building was £700 over and above the free labour given.

The result in Eriskay was a small jewel of vernacular ecclesiastical architecture. The spare and solid masonry of its exterior concealed an inside which was bathed from dawn to dusk in unpolluted Hebridean light. The rafters of the new St Michael's Church resembled the ribs of a broad ship turned upside down. Other nautical references would be incorporated as the century progressed – a bell from the German battlecruiser SMS *Derfflinger*, which was scuttled while interned at Scapa Flow in the Orkney islands in 1919, was mounted outside, and the bow of a lifeboat washed overboard from the post-World War II British aircraft carrier HMS *Hermes* was remodelled and placed under the altar – but it is probable that nothing could have added to the original purity of St Michael's Church in Eriskay when it was completed in 1903.

The building was consecrated on 7 May in the same year. Nine priests travelled to Eriskay for the occasion. A contingent of four from the western mainland, which included Father Allan's cousin Sandy MacKintosh from Fort William, was headed by Bishop George Smith. Five island priests from South Uist, Barra and

Benbecula were also present. Allan MacDonald stood among them for a group photograph with his hands clasped behind his back; tall, proud and happy.

But the party was as notable for its absentees as for its members. Three of his friends, fellow San Ambrosians and Gaels, were not there who should have been in Eriskay to share Father Allan's gladness. Five months earlier, at the turn of the year, Father James Chisholm from Strathglass – who was by then the Very Reverend Canon James Chisholm – had left Barra after 20 years in the island to work in the western mainland parish of Arisaig.

Shortly after Canon Chisholm's arrival in Arisaig, Father Donald MacLellan died a few miles away in North Morar. The South Uist boy from Kilphedar whose poor health had obliged him to leave his friends in Valladolid ahead of schedule, but who had nonetheless completed his studies in Scotland, been ordained and moved back to minister in the Gaidhealtachd, contracted infected peritonitis in January 1903 and passed away within days of taking to his bed. His sister Catherine was at his side. He was 48 years old.

Two months later, at 6.30 a.m. on 15 March 1903, the big heart of Father John MacKintosh stopped beating. Sagart Mor nan Each had left the horses and hunting of South Uist for Campbeltown in mainland Argyllshire in 1900. His departure from Bornish was marked by a celebration at which Father Allan read out one of his famously unsparing bardic tributes. Father John had a couple of years on the west coast seaboard before the Bright's disease, or chronic nephritis, which had troubled him for years took its final toll. Sagart Mor nan Each began to cough up blood. There was no effective treatment and no cure. He died in the Campbeltown priest's house. He was 43 years old.

Father Allan MacDonald was also 43 years old in that bittersweet year. In 1903 the average life expectancy of British men was 47 years. As a priest knew better than most, in the Highlands and Islands of Scotland it was slightly less than that.

There would be no more hilarious reminiscences over Spanish wine in Castlebay and Bornish, no more jokes at the expense of visiting English Jesuits, no more laughing until 'I've had to go outside and knock my head against the wall'. In one direction or another, his generation had moved on. Allan MacDonald understood, as he showed his bishop the new St Michael's Church in May 1903, that he would be going nowhere. He had already pointed to the place of his burial. It was down on the thin green sward by the sands of western Eriskay.

But he had work still to do. In 1903 he obtained special permission from the Vatican to say Mass on one of the Eriskay fishing boats every year in the month of May, introducing a Mediterranean tradition to the Hebrides.

> The fishermen at his request thoroughly cleansed out their boats and gave them the names of Saints. He then gathered them together and blessed them. They cast lots to decide on what boat Mass would be celebrated. An altar with a canopy overhead was erected on the lucky boat, and the others gathered in a circle round it, all gaily festooned and decorated with flags and banners. Some of the flags came from as far away as Hammersmith, others were provided by the fishermen owners.

His admiration for the Eriskay fishermen was boundless. He said once,

> It would be hard to find anywhere men better pleased with their lives than these poor fishermen. You'll see them out all night in a storm, coming up from the boats in the morning with a song in their mouths. Their poor wives will have been up on the hillside since before daylight looking out for them, and when the men come up singing and joking, they say, 'Here we are breaking our hearts – and you're quite pleased!' ...
>
> I've often watched one of them in a rough sea, baiting lines at the gunwale, both hands engaged, upright without effort and unconcerned, balancing himself with the very bottom of

his boat standing up against the back of him ... There was a man who had been a deep-sea sailor came here once, and they didn't like to have him around, for he was always falling overboard.

He wrote a Gaelic 'Fisherman's Hymn' especially for his people. He kept an oil lamp burning at night by the altar in the new St Michael's, high up on Rubha Ban, for the benefit of his seafaring men. 'I like to think they can be seeing this,' he said.

Father Allan's life early in the new century was not all death and departure. In 1904, after ten years back home in the English midlands, Frederick Rea returned to Garrynamonie School. Rea wasted little time in taking his sister to visit his old friend in Eriskay. Their boat sailed from Polachar in South Uist to Haun, where

Ascending from the south shore of the little bay we came in sight of the newly built church and priest's house.

A tall black figure standing there began to descend the hill towards us as we climbed – it was Father Allan. His face broke into a kindly smile as he approached us and extended his hand in welcome. 'Come up to my house,' he said after I had introduced my sister. Then he turned to her with: 'It is a rough way up. We did make a road from here to my house, but the hens scratched it up,' and I saw a twinkle in his eye as he said it.

While Frederick Rea's sister browsed through Father Allan's library the two men walked outside. Rea then pointed over the sound to northern Barra. Rea recounted how

I told him that I had been out in my garden a few nights previously, before retiring to rest, and stood for a moment looking across to the sea, when I saw a dull-lighted sphere hovering over that part of the island I had indicated. At first I thought: 'How curious the moon looks tonight!' But as I was looking, I saw the sphere of dim light rise very slowly into the air. I watched it go up steadily, higher, higher, and disappear into the sky.

'Oh, I have often seen it myself...' said Father Allan. 'Sometimes I have been fetched in a boat to [a] dying person and when the boat has been perhaps half-way, I have said to the men: "You can put back, for we are too late", for I had seen the ascending light. I have never been mistaken yet over this... Some people have the gift of being enabled to see what is denied to others.'

In 1904 a Dundonian artist named John Duncan also arrived in Eriskay. Duncan had been lecturing in Celtic Art at the University of Chicago. He returned to Scotland in 1903 determined to master the Gaelic language and study Gaelic culture. In his mid 30s he discovered in the southern Outer Hebrides, especially Eriskay, a 'holy quiet'. Eriskay should be approached, he wrote, 'clad in peace and shod in silence. One should dawn into it and fade from it without hail or farewell.' John Duncan, who wrote much as he painted, also detected the presence in Barra and Eriskay of fairies. 'I am not mad,' he insisted. 'I know they are not to be confused with mortal men and women. They do not collide with solid bodies but they are not shape-shifters. Nothing ghostlike or vaporous...'

John Duncan was a friend of Marjory Kennedy-Fraser and was directly responsible for enticing that formidable lady to the Hebrides. A Perthshire woman who was born into a musical family and brought up in Edinburgh and London, Kennedy-Fraser enjoyed a good, international singing career at the end of the nineteenth century. She was not a Gaelic speaker, but when she was in her 20s in the early 1880s she came across the traditional Gaelic airs which had been published by Logan & Co. of Inverness, and added two or three of them to her repertoire. Twenty years later she embarked on a lucrative crusade to collect, clean up, rearrange and rewrite in English for a drawing-room audience as many Gaelic songs and tunes as she could find. If she could not find them, she made them up. Her collection would later be described by Anne Lorne Gillies, a real authority on Gaelic music, as 'a curate's egg in which the authentic is infuriatingly difficult to disentangle from the romanticised ramblings and reinventions'.

In 1904 John Duncan wrote to tell Marjory Kennedy-Fraser that he had 'discovered' the island of Eriskay, and it was the perfect spot for them both. 'He knew', she wrote, 'that I had long dreamed of doing original research work in Celtic music . . . He instantly wrote to me thence that this was the place, and that come out there I must, and that speedily.'

She arrived 'wet, sick and weary' at Lochboisdale pier the following August. Duncan met her there and took her immediately to Eriskay. After supper at her lodgings in the main village below the new church, John Duncan escorted a little local girl into the house and sat her on Kennedy-Fraser's knee. The tot then sang Gaelic songs. 'I had sailed, I felt,' said Kennedy-Fraser, 'out of the twentieth century back at least into the 1600s.'

John Duncan painted in Eriskay while Marjory Kennedy-Fraser strolled around the island with the musical equivalent of a butterfly net. Duncan made a dramatic landscape of a funeral party: a coffin being sailed from Eriskay to South Uist while on the shore men and women huddled in prayer and Father Allan, in a white surplice, knelt erect in their midst; as tall on his knees, the painter suggested, as some of the mourners would be on their feet.

Kennedy-Fraser made her own delighted observations. Eriskay had, she noted,

No fences, no roads (with the exception of the footpath), no carts, no wheelbarrows even; burdens of all kinds were carried, exposed to the view of the interested onlooker, in creels on the backs of the people, or in panniers on the flanks of the Barra ponies.

Sometimes the load would be seaweed for manure; or a particular kind of seaweed which they spread on the rocks out of reach of the sea till, sweetened by the rain and sun, it is fit to be used for bedding, and very good mattresses it makes. The peats, too, had to be carried in creels or in the horse-panniers, and heather had to be fetched from a distance as there was none on the island; so boats could be seen leaving early in the morning for South Uist to fetch bracken and heather for thatching; and, returning the same night, men and women could be seen with the laden creels, toiling up the slope with their burdens, and storing the stuff in byres, against the needful re-thatching of the cottage roof.

At all hours of the day children and old wives and maidens were to be seen herding, for in an unfenced world everybody's cow was always getting into everybody else's corn, and at any hour an excited chase might be seen, when some four-footed feeder got into forbidden pasture.

Then the boats, with their graceful brown wings, were a feature of the Monday mornings, going out to the fishing, and again, on the Saturdays, returning. Occasionally a boat went round to Lochboisdale with barrels of fish or the like, and returned with stores; and although every morning Father Allan MacDonald held service in the little chapel on the hill, it was on Sunday mornings that the whole island turned out. Then a long procession of women, young and old, of bairns, and of great, dark, brawny men, might be seen climbing up the hill, as Father Allan came out of his presbytery, and himself tolled the bell which called them to worship.

The disciplined philologist and folklorist in Allan MacDonald cannot entirely have approved of this English speaker cherry-picking in his culture. He even criticised the National Mod, the annual showcase of Gaelic song and verse which had been established in Oban in 1891, for its distortions and simplifications – Gaelic songs typically heard at the Mod were, he said, 'As though you were to fit a statue into a box by taking off the nose and ears'. But his own manuscript collection was long gone, to Edinburgh and the safekeeping of Walter Blaikie, and he showed Marjory Kennedy-Fraser his usual courtesy. She was hot on the trail of one man whom she called Gillespie,* 'a young fisher, quiet in manner and dark and rather handsome in appearance, [who] had songs that were not known to others'.

On the Monday morning before she left Eriskay, Kennedy-Fraser realised with alarm that she had failed to make a transcription of what she would call 'The Skye Fisher's Song' from the quiet, dark, handsome fisherman.

> There was no time to be lost. I set out before breakfast to his mother's house, a long, oblong, old-fashioned hut, standing back from the beach where Prince Charlie landed in 1745 ... Gillespie's mother came to the door when I knocked, and kindly bid me 'Thig a stigh.' I had enough Gaelic to know that I was asked to walk in ... She sat me down on a low, three-legged stool by the peat fire which was burning brightly on the floor, and seated herself on another ...
>
> The interior of the old hut was really beautiful in the morning light, which slanted down from the small, deep-set windows on the dear old woman by the fire, who did not appear to regard my early visit as an intrusion, but cheerfully and promptly set herself to entertain me. She had no English, and I had little conversational Gaelic, so we sang Gaelic songs to one another, and she was pleased, and with Highland politeness said that I had 'Gaidhlig gu leor'.
>
> But by-and-bye the old man came in, and he told me that Gillespie was already out in the boat, which was lying at anchor in the harbour, and that he would be mending nets till midday, when they were to set sail. This was getting serious. I wanted that tune. So I went to Father Allan with my tale of woe, and he listened with a glint of humour and sympathy in his eyes, and said 'Come with me.'

---

* Gilleasbuig: an original Gaelic name which is anglicised as Archibald.

I trotted by his side – he was a tall, spare man – down from the presbytery on the rock to the little harbour, and by the door of the small store – there was only one store in the place where you could sometimes get bread, but oftener couldn't for love or money – by the door leant Dugald of the post-office and the clerk who attended to the sales. Father Allan gave them orders to take me out in a small boat to the fishing-smack, where we would find Gillespie at his nets.

The store was locked at once, the two men got a boat, and handing me off the slippery seaweed-covered rocks in the low tide, rowed me out to the harbour. Gillespie was busy with his nets, and they chaffed him, I could see, about the strange lady who was running after him for his singing. So I had to wait about half an hour before he would be persuaded to sing, although the men urged him with 'Suas leis an oran'. He continued mending his brown nets in the glorious morning sunlight, with the purple sea lying quiet round us. But at last he yielded, and having once begun, sang verse after verse, and I got it noted down.

Thus was Father Allan MacDonald responsible – 'with a glint of humour in his eyes' – for 'The Skye Fisher's Song' and 'The Mull Fisher's Love Song', as well perhaps as 'An Eriskay Love Lilt' and 'An Eriskay Lullaby'. His friends and admirers occasionally had good reason to wish that he was more possessive of his sources. As she left Eriskay early one morning in 1905, Marjory Kennedy-Fraser looked back. 'The last thing I noted', she recalled, 'as we drew away from the shore was the tall, spare figure of Father Allan (the Lord of the Isles, they called him*) coming out from the door of his presbytery on the rock and crossing to the little chapel which commanded the harbour.'

Allan MacDonald had a surfeit of people discovering him and

---

* This actually was another of Father Allan's local nicknames and not a lift from Neil Munro's novel. He was aware of it, and referred to the British mainland as 'the Adjoining Kingdom'.

his island in 1905. Kennedy-Fraser and John Duncan had been in a party of five which also included the young Aberdeen poet Rachel Annand Taylor. Earlier in the year Father Allan had hosted the American musician Evelyn Benedict, who had been a member of the artistic community on Appledore Island, a few acres of bare rock off the east coast of Maine.

On the heels of Evelyn Benedict and Marjory Kennedy-Fraser, Amy Murray landed at Haun.

Amy Murray was 41 years old in 1905. She was a native of Goshen in New York State. Miss Murray was a notable beauty, comparable in appearance to the shapely American actress and singer Lillian Russell, a fact which would have made the men of Eriskay, accustomed as they were by 1905 to Father Allan's elegant lady visitors, pay extra attention. But Amy Murray was there only for one of them.

She was descended on her father's side from a Scot who had reputedly deserted from the British Army during the American Revolution, married a Dutch girl and settled down in Orange County. Amy had great musical ability and from a young age sang in choirs and performed semi-professionally at the salons and society gatherings of New York. In her 30s she became anxious to discover her roots and crossed the Atlantic to Britain. She learned some Gaelic and travelled around the Highlands and Inner Hebrides. Upon returning to New York she began to lecture on and give recitals of 'Scottish and Gaelic Folk-Song', accompanying herself on the harp. In 1905 she returned to Scotland to pursue the Gaelic music which would become her lifelong passion. This time Amy Murray was advised by the Cornish scholar Henry Jenner to visit Father Allan MacDonald in the Outer Hebridean island of Eriskay. Jenner's recommendation was echoed when she met Alexander Carmichael in Edinburgh. 'Tell Father Allan you are my friend,' said Carmichael.

She landed at Lochboisdale in South Uist in the middle of August 1905, to the distressing news that Father Allan was away in the north of the islands. She lodged overnight with the nuns at the Bute Hospital in Daliburgh. On the following day, a Saturday, Allan MacDonald drove back from the north in a gig to the priest's house in Daliburgh, where he was relieving the incumbent during the latter's summer holiday. A nun at the Bute Hospital sent word down the road to St Peter's that Miss Amy Murray had appeared among them. Father Allan sent back the request for 'Miss Murray [to] be so good as to come up to him – he being so very tired.' So she did.

> When Father Allan opened the door to me, I saw the red of a good peat-fire at his back. He stood up tall against it, straight and lean, with that lift of the head and that glint in the eye that seem to say – before one is saying anything – 'Well, here are you, and here am I!' ... A fair man, and greying a little, clean-shaven of course, weather-beaten, high-cheek-boned, the lower lip the least bit to the fore.
>
> For a breath I had the sense that I was taken in from top to toe ... Then, 'I heard you were on your way!' With this, bowing a little as he took my hand gently into one agreeably smooth and warm, he brought me in and put me down at one side the fire, himself at the other.
>
> So this was Father Allan ...
>
> Plenty light still came in at the window, nine o'clock and after though it was; the soft flattering twilight of summer in high latitudes; whereby, with the peat-glow to help it, his face showed somewhat younger and a trifle fairer than I was to see it later by the light of day.

She had expected to find an 'old and broken' priest. She discovered instead a paragon –

> a man more than mannerly, a man with an air of the Great World itself; barely middle-aged ... flat of back and square of shoulder, quick-moving, light-stepping, his head carried

high ... Could there be some mistake? What if this were not Father Allan after all? ...

All this (and more) went buzzing through my head, while I was answering his [queries]. How were our friends? and, How was I? and bearing as I could my part in the talk that ran on lightly, never halting, ranging from 'Fiona Macleod'* and the Celtic Gloom to the house we sat in, and the wall he had himself put round it and the chapel to keep the pigs out ... 'I couldn't stand a pig coming in while I was saying Mass!'

This must be Father Allan, then, I reassured myself ... And I thought as I listened, I'd never heard speech I liked better (English of the best, with a certain richness to the turn of it that was not altogether English), nor words coming faster from the lips of man nor woman; nor seen such a face for looks of young and old together. Such a likable mingling, too, of manly Highland traits; pride, sensitiveness, humour, warm-heartedness and latent sternness; the whole much sweetened by a smile that warmed his keen eyes wonderfully.

Light-blue, quick-glancing, the eyes of a man and a masterful one, the least bit puckered at the outer corners as a sailor's are, these gave promise of seeing far across the water as any man's in Eriskay – as indeed they could. Shaggy brows overhung them, greying like his hair (close-cropped after fisherman-fashion, with a lock left to show below the cap-brim) and these worked about while he spoke or while he listened.

Greyish-fair, well-weathered was his colour altogether. His age had already puzzled better guessers than myself. Only a few

---

* William Sharp was a Paisley man who in the 1890s took to writing Celtic romances which were published under the nom de plume of 'Fiona MacLeod'. They were littered with faux-Gaelic references which pleased a southern readership but which experts such as Allan MacDonald instantly recognised as fakery. Sharp went to great lengths to conceal his true identity – dictating letters to his sister so that they had a woman's handwriting – and despite being the cause of much debate and speculation 'Fiona MacLeod' was not publicly unmasked until after his death in December 1905.

days before at Lochmaddy he had asked a man, 'How old am I?' After a long look and a long thought, the man – who was reckoned a judge of such matters – had ventured, 'Anywhere between thirty-five and seventy.'

He was in fact just past his six-and-fortieth birthday,* and had been for one-and-twenty years a priest on the True Edge of the Great World.

Allan MacDonald took to Amy Murray almost as much as she took to him. 'I could not but mark how more and more his tone grew friendly,' she said, 'his look, at first somewhat aloof (as any priest's will be in face of woman), now dwelling openly on mine; while now and again he spoke of work we were to do together.'

She stayed with him for almost six weeks, until the last days of September 1905. That first evening he brought a Uist piper into the Daliburgh priest's house, 'And grand piping he gave us that night! Reels – marches – gatherings – strathspeys, – the walls were like to burst. Pushing back the chairs, Seumas took the floor's length to his treading and his turning; and all the while Father Allan's foot kept time, while now and again we would hear a loud "Hooch!" out of him.'

Father Allan was to return to Eriskay on the following afternoon. As he had other visitors it was agreed that Miss Murray would join him there a few days later. He had noted her elaborate Edwardian headware. 'Eriskay is no place for hats,' he said. She returned late that night to the nuns at Bute Hospital. Next morning she walked with one of the sisters back again to Sunday Mass at St Peter's to find,

> ... five or six hundred here already ... All the benches are filled, saving space for us two at the front; when we come out again, we are to find late-comers kneeling on the flag-stones in the porch.

---

* He was 45 years old.

We are late ourselves, it seems. Directly we have knelt, a round-faced little fellow with a taper held tight in his two hands comes out to light the altar.

Slowly, genuflecting with reverent awkwardness, his coarse boots clattering on the bare boards, he kindles one by one the little orange-yellow flames that fling and flicker in the salt breeze from the open window, whereon floats in a drift of peat-reek from a black house near.

Within, the air is heavy with that same peat-savour, clinging in the woollen shawls and jerseys. Scraping the boards as they shift uneasily in their cramped sittings and kneelings, they breathe hard, sigh loudly, the poor crofter-fisher-folk; while from here and there I hear the cough that comes of the long chilly nights in the boats, the long wet days at the herding . . .

And now the little server, having set the last flame leaping, crooks himself in the last of his reverences and tramps loudly out. Then in by another door comes Father Allan; a stately man and an upstanding in his chasuble of faded red; an older man by morning light, and greyer, his look aloof and stern. Now with a lad at either side of him he kneels at the first step of the altar, and uplifts the Prayer before the Mass:

'O Iosa! a Mhic an De Bheo . . .'

'(O Jesus! Son of the God of Life . . .)

in a voice that his speech of last night hardly hinted – a voice that has surely not its like in London.

To the relief and satisfaction of each of them, Amy Murray arrived in Eriskay on Wednesday of that week. She was given a guest room at the priest's house on Am Rubha Ban and put into the expert care of Penelope Campbell – she 'was always thinking on what next she could be giving me, always searching her brains for somewhat I might "mark down".' Penelope Campbell also approved of Miss Murray's hats.

When he made time to enjoy it, Allan MacDonald revelled in the company of this charming American. Three days into her visit – presumably on Saturday –

... and we on our way towards the glen, Father Allan called out to a man delving his potato-patch, 'What weather will we have?... We call him "the prophet",' he added in my ear.

'Seven days of sunshine,' gave back 'the prophet' promptly, whereat we laughed. Seven days of sunshine nevertheless we had.

We behove to make the most of them. So one day saw us on the one way of the path, the next day on the other, another day taking our own way; and Father Allan always talking, talking – always seeing folk and faces in the clouds ... There was never a tint in the sea nor the sky but he was marking it and naming it; and many the rann [verse] and the bit of old song that he'd have in his mouth. Half as to himself and half to me, one day of these I heard him murmuring:

'Where many the sowings of storms;
Where few the sowings of seed.'

He took Miss Murray with him on some of his parish duties.

Four times in the year Father Allan carried the Sacrament to the infirm and aged, and I had come just before his midsummer rounds. Two mornings would make them. We behove to take our porridge early, for sake of the old people who would be fasting till he came ...

Most days, then, he goes about like the fishermen in darkblue serge, with a deer-stalker cap and a belted jacket, his trousers tucked into the tops of stout boots, and only the cut of his collar to show him in orders. But to-day a black coat covers him and a black hat too, which latter he takes care to pull well down as we set out; since, for all the sun's shining, the wind seems nowise minded we should be forgetting him.

And indeed, where the path climbs a boulder to spare a barley-patch, he fetches me such a buffet as makes me glad to catch at Father Allan's hand – always ready, as though he were used to the squiring of women.

There was an unmistakably chaste and slightly one-sided romance in that summer of 1905. Father Allan MacDonald would not have needed constantly to remind himself that he was a priest. But Miss Amy Murray did.

We are stooping to enter the first doorway when a sound of chanting halts us.

Where we are, then, we stand, and Father Allan bares his head, while I look past his shoulder into a dark chamber of some depth, its floor freshly strewn with white sand. A little to left of the middle, two or three peats send up a slender stream of reek. Coiling and thinning as it rises, it drifts and hangs among the sooty rafters overhead, settles down in the corners thick and brown.

Daylight from a little window to the North strikes out a band of cloudy blue across it, just above the head of a young dark-haired woman who kneels facing us, her baby in her arms. Two little girls cling one at either side; and where these were getting eyes blue as the Coolins in clear weather, and fringed like the peat-pools in Uist, it's easy seeing.

Since early morning they were on the watch, that the priest might find them kneeling thus and chanting, 'I am not worthy, O Lord! that Thou shouldst enter here.'

Father Allan goes ... where a cailleach lies bed-fast; the young woman follows with the children at her heels, their faces buried in her skirts for bashfulness; and I, well content, seat myself by the fire on the floor, where two little sleepy cats sit nodding, and a pot hangs bubbling from the roof.

Amy Murray sent to Edinburgh for her harp. 'You'll never be able to keep a string on it here,' said Father Allan. He was wrong. It arrived in its box in a rowing boat and was bundled over the slippery rocks.

I harped and sang indoors that day and night to Father Allan and [Penelope Campbell] ... Next morning again we were at it ... though the iron braces of its box went red with rust; though I played it so often out before the door, to the people standing round, that Father Allan gave the rock I used to sit on the name of Creag na Chlarsaich – the Rock of the Harp; though I had it in black houses at ceilidh before a peat-fire of a fervour to melt the pins of it, and out on Rudha Ban to let the wind finger the strings, – for all that, in all that time four strings were all I broke.

'And how would it be sounding on the rocks down by the water?' Father Allan wondered. We tried that out the first fine day.

Under his guidance, week after week Amy Murray collected the songs of Eriskay. 'We're a humorous people,' he told her, 'better take us while we're in the humour.' She took down songs in their houses from young girls and old women, and songs from the fishermen at their nets. She wrote down songs at ceilidhs and songs from women waulking tweed. 'A great deal of these people's singing is nothing more to them than just a way of doing [things],' said her host. 'When they come up to tell me of anyone dying or in trouble, they always chant it.'

'I went once to tell a fisherman's wife that her husband was drowned,' Father Allan told her. 'She was in bed ... "Och, you needn't tell me your errand!" she said; "I know that Angus is drowned."'

'I took her hands in mine – there was nothing I could say. She raised herself up, and burst out into a chant – three verses of poetry. Then she shook her head a little from side to side, and fell back in a swoon. I saw this again at a funeral. It was at Christmas, and the dead was a young girl. The coffin was on the stakes and they were lifting it; the mother bent over it and burst out into chanting and singing – several lines of beautiful verse. They said to her afterwards, "What did you say?" ... and she had no memory of it.'

'"Instinct right, reflection wrong, / When you get a man to sing a song",' he said. She listened and noted, and thought that she was hearing music from the beginning of time. 'I haven't the folk-song sound in my voice,' he said. 'I didn't learn the songs when I was young, and now I can't make them folky.' But he made sure she got the lyrics right.

They rushed together like children out of the door of the priest's house to watch rainbows in the daytime and moonbows at night. He told her that you cannot find a place nearer to Heaven on earth than Eriskay.

When Amy Murray's time came to leave, shortly before St Michael's Day on 29 September 1905, Father Allan MacDonald sailed with her across the sound to Polachar in South Uist. He put her into the two-wheeled cart which would take her to the pierhead at Lochboisdale and the steamer south.

They shook hands over the side of the cart. 'Send me the songs,' he said. She began to say something in return but he cut her short. 'Never mind about that,' he said. 'Only send me the songs.'

A fortnight later Amy Murray went into the town centre of Stirling to buy a blank music book and begin the proper transcription of her songs collected in Eriskay.

She was told there that Father Allan was dead.

OCTOBER 1905

Despite appearances, Father Allan had never recovered full health after his breakdown in 1892. He told his diary in Eriskay repeatedly that he was 'seedy', 'exhausted' and 'unable to do anything', and that 'my paleness and emaciation [is] attracting attention'. He had tried drinking coffee instead of tea, cutting back on his pipe-smoking and drinking porter, without feeling much better.

He was right: other people had noticed. In September 1895 the Church of Scotland minister Peter Dewar wrote to the Marquess of Bute to say: 'I am most sincerely sorry to hear that the state of the health of the Revd A Macdonald of Eriskay is thought to be so serious, for he has thrown himself heart and soul into the work of his sacred calling, and is a man of fine qualities of head and heart.'

Penelope Campbell had reluctantly refrained from reporting to him the drunken misdemeanours of some Eriskay fishermen because they 'were no kind of doings for a man with a bad heart'. Amy Murray had been warned by Henry Jenner in 1905 that 'Some little doubt was of [Father Allan's] welfare, he being a man much broken by his work.'

Shortly after putting Miss Murray into the cart at Polachar he went down with what was thought to be influenza. It quickly turned into pneumonia and – his doctor considered – pleurisy. His tired heart gave out in the priest's house at Am Rubha Ban on Sunday, 8 October 1905. He was 45 years old. His brother Ronald crossed the Minch from Glenshiel in time to sign the death certificate.

Father Allan MacDonald's death was reported and regretted nationally. His loss, said the *Glasgow News*, 'will be profoundly felt, not only amongst the people of the barren little community to whom he was priest and king, but by many people in many parts who interest themselves in Celtic history and folk-lore. Father Allan Macdonald was a most interesting and loveable personality.'

'Beloved in a special degree,' said the *Oban Times*, 'by his own communion far and wide, he held a peculiar place of regard in the hearts of all who knew him – and indeed of many who had only heard of him – by reason of his high ideals, his single-eyed devotion to the welfare of others, his scholarship, and his outlook upon life.'

'When Father Allan died,' wrote Reverend George Henderson in the *Celtic Review*, ' . . . there passed away from the Highlands one who was possessed in a double measure of the spirit of his race, from the world one of its nobles. His many-sided virtues it would be impossible to praise too highly, and the aptness of his mind for story, and fun, and wit.'

The *Catholic Directory* said

> In temporal matters, he was at [his people's] service as a leader and adviser. In an acute crisis regarding the land question, he guided his people wisely and well, in their successful struggle to obtain fixity and more reasonable conditions of tenure . . . The houses were improved, bridle paths made where there are no roads nor ever have been by the Congested Districts Board. Once a year he solemnly blessed the Eriskay fishing fleet and, by special permission of the Pope, said Mass on one of the boats to bring God's blessing on men and boats and fishing gear, 'ere starting on the season's work.
>
> Notwithstanding his busy life and impaired health, he was an indefatigable student of Gaelic and a recognised authority on all that related to traditions, whether Celtic or Norse, the folk-lore, fairy tales, antiquities and history, the fauna and flora, the shells and algae of the Hebrides . . . Father Allan

may some day be given the place among Celtic scholars which by every right is his. He gave all too freely be it said of his gleanings to other workers in the Celtic field.

'A life of extraordinary devotion to others,' said the *Scotsman*, 'and of unceasing self-sacrifice has been extinguished, and a rich repository of Celtic folk-lore disappears ... In his own Church he was held in high honour; but far beyond the Roman Catholic communion he had countless admirers and affectionate friends. To know Father Allan was to love him.'

Twenty-one priests, many friends and the whole of the island of Eriskay attended his funeral service at and outside the church that he had built on Am Rubha Ban. He had earlier cleared of nettles and fenced with driftwood a small patch of machair by the western shore. 'Let me be buried amongst my dead and near to my living people, that I may be near them, and that they and I may rise together at the Last Day,' he decreed.

So his coffin was carried down from Am Rubha Ban to the freshly cut grave facing the Sound of Barra. The visiting clergy followed the coffin-bearers, and behind them came 'the women and children, children on foot and children in arms, mothers and their families weeping and praying for the fond father who was making his last journey to his home in their midst; the aged too, men and women all took part in that last act of veneration to one they loved so well.'

One tradition may have died on that day. A young boy who had been taken from Barra to Father Allan's funeral in Eriskay would remember much later that he never again heard keening in the Hebrides. 'That was the last time he heard the women keening, you know, wailing.'

When Father Allan's coffin was lowered into its grave, the diggers took up their spades to fill it in again. They were eased aside by the people of Eriskay. Four hundred men, women and children then took handfuls of soil and sods and sand, and gently filled in the grave themselves.

NOTES

CHAPTER ONE : THE POST-HORN

p.3   'full charged to the muzzle, . . . off the road' *The Cruise of the Betsey*, Hugh Miller, 1868

p.5   'was closely acquainted with everyone . . . lightened their journey for them' John N. MacLeod, *Stornoway Gazette*, 27 October 1933

p.11   'There is not an instance . . . the most extraordinary kind' *A Tour of Scotland, Volume II*, Thomas Pennant, 1774

pp.11–12 'Peace reigns in Fort William now . . . wonderfully picturesque surroundings' *In Far Lochaber*, William Black, 1888

CHAPTER TWO: THE STRANGE LIFE OF CATHOLIC SCOTLAND

p.20   'the severity of the penal laws . . . done with much greater freedom' Alexander Winster, quoted in *A History of the Catholic Church in Scotland*, Alphons Bellesheim, 1890

p.21   'The preservation of the faith . . . fled before the tempest, but had remained faithful at his post' *A History of the Catholic Church in Scotland*, Alphons Bellesheim, 1890

p.22   'if the laird was Protestant . . . the people Catholic' Rev. John Cameron, *Evidence taken by Her Majesty's Commissioners of Inquiry into the conditions of the crofters and cottars in the Highlands and Islands of Scotland, Volume III*, London, 1884

p.24   'enjoying peace . . . being added to the Church' *A History of the Catholic Church in Scotland*, Alphons Bellesheim, 1890

p.24   'the first Jacobite rising . . . verge of disappearing from the country' *A History of the Catholic Church in Scotland*, Alphons Bellesheim, 1890 p.30   'In countries lying . . . to strengthen that interest' Report of Messrs Hyndman and Dick to the General Assembly of the Church of Scotland, 1760

p.31   'To have exterminated . . . but incomparably more politic' *Constitutional History of England*, Henry Hallam, 1827

p.33   'There still continues in Scotland . . . the protection of wise governments' *Caledonia*, George Chalmers, 1810

p.36   'religion is the most important . . . the life of the child' Letter of Pope Gregory XVI to Irish Bishops, 1831

p.39   'the barns and byres . . . the familiar name of Coll' *Catholic Directory*, 1891

CHAPTER THREE: BLAIRS

p.44   'Fr Allan was heard . . . seem luxurious by comparison' *Father Allan McDonald of Eriskay*, John Lorne Campbell, 1954

p.44   'a man of keen intellect . . . singleness of purpose' *Memorial of Centenary of St Mary's College, Blairs*, Mgr John Ritchie, 1929

p.44   A place where life . . . that monster Homer!' *Eilein na h-Oige, The Poems of Fr Allan McDonald*, Ronald Black (ed.), 2002

p.45   'geography . . . and divinity' *Memorial of Centenary of St Mary's College, Blairs*, Mgr John Ritchie, 1929

p.45   'He had no liking for Greek . . . nor for philosophy' George Henderson, *Celtic Review*, January 1906

p.47   'He's a hunter . . . a blast from the deep throat of a trombone' *Eilein na h-Oige, The Poems of Fr Allan McDonald*, Ronald Black (ed.), 2002

CHAPTER FOUR: VALLADOLID

p.50   'ill-prepared . . . for their work' *The Scots College in Spain*, Maurice Taylor, 1971

p.51   'Scottish by birth . . . aforesaid conversion may require' ibid.

p.52   'the excessive cold . . . of the summer' Rev. David MacDonald, quoted in *The Scots College in Spain*, Maurice Taylor, 1971

p.53   'I found this college . . . between us on religious matters' *The Bible in Spain*, George Borrow, 1843 p.54 'Day of barricades . . . at least in public churches' Rev. David MacDonald, quoted in *The Scots College in Spain*, Maurice Taylor, 1971

pp.55–6 'Many a time . . . sighed privately, "Lord save us from scrupulous Rectors"' *The Scots College in Spain*, Maurice Taylor, 1971

p.56 'Neither the college . . . I am at all happy here' ibid.

p.57 'strong-willed, energetic . . . a complete lack of tact' *Father Archangel of Scotland and other essays*, Gabriela Cunninghame Graham, 1896

p.58 'go into villages . . . any kind of fruit to the house' *The Scots College in Spain*, Maurice Taylor, 1971

p.59 'Day sunny but cool . . . The company departed around three o'clock' ibid.

p.59 'a special tea . . . and finally cards' ibid.

p.60 'For is it not in preaching . . . our Alma Mater.' ibid.

pp.60–1 'We spent a while . . . as was proper for us . . .' *Eilein na h-Oige, The Poems of Fr Allan McDonald*, Ronald Black (ed), 2002

p.62 'The Right Rev. Angus Macdonald . . . such manifold activities' *The Catholic Highlands of Scotland*, Odo Blundell, 1917

p.65 'That little firebrand . . . by an *argumentum a posteriori*' *The Scots College in Spain*, Maurice Taylor, 1971

CHAPTER FIVE: OBAN

p.67 'very well satisfied . . . impediment, except want of age' Report of examiners, 1882, Scottish Catholic Archive

p.70 'by the end of June . . . a general air of bustle and of coming and going' *Ordnance Gazetteer of Scotland, 1882–1885*

p.71 'We in Barra here . . . belong to our own denomination' *Evidence taken by Her Majesty's Commissioners of Inquiry into the conditions of the crofters and cottars in the Highlands and Islands of Scotland*, Volume I, London, 1884

pp.72–3 'I refer . . . deterred by fear from exercising that right' *Evidence taken by Her Majesty's Commissioners of Inquiry into the conditions of the crofters and cottars in the Highlands and Islands of Scotland*, Appendix, London, 1884

CHAPTER SIX: SOUTH UIST

p.76   'We can learn to appreciate . . . elders of the district' *The Catholic Highlands of Scotland*, Odo Blundell, 1917

p.77   'It's a nasty day, this! . . . Well, it's not his best, then' *Father Allan's Island*, Amy Murray, 1918

p.77   'Free-Kirkers have the name . . . a genial man withal, and a well-liked' ibid.

p.77   'No Gloom, then . . . striding round amongst them' ibid.

p.78   'It would be satisfactory . . . needed where one is isolated' Allan MacDonald's journal, unpublished

p.78   'very small middle class . . . schoolmasters and government officials' preface to *A School in South Uist*, Frederick Rea, 1964

p.79   'above the middle-size . . . a hardy constitution' *An Early Scottish Traveller in Egypt (In Search of John Gordon, 1804)*, Roger O. De Keersmaecker, 1998

p.81   'The Uist people . . . Nature's noblemen' *Carmina Gadelica, Ortha nan Gaidheal*, Introduction to Vol. I, Alexander Carmichael, 1900

p.81   'Sometimes he would come . . . seal-shooting with the landlord . . .' *A School in South Uist*, Frederick Rea, 1964

p.82   'we slackened pace . . . Alasdair said: "Lady Cathcart . . .!"' ibid.

p.83   'How simple it would be . . . rights as crofters would be forfeited' Allan MacDonald's journal, unpublished

pp.83–4   'I beg to ask . . . against the closing of a valuable chemical trade?' *Hansard*, 21 July 1890

pp.84–5   'poverty, misery, neglect . . . almost inhospitable, discourteous' *Outer Isles*, Ada Goodrich Freer, 1903

pp.85–6   'We were not allowed to keep a dog . . . caught by authorised officers' *Evidence taken by Her Majesty's Commissioners of Inquiry into the conditions of the crofters and cottars in the Highlands and Islands of Scotland*, Volume I, London, 1884

p.86   'When I was a young man . . . today there is very little' ibid.

pp.86–7   'I saw a policeman . . . Let him alone. It is against the law" ibid.

p.87   'the clearances in 1851 . . . to exaggerate would not be easy'
        *Evidence taken by Her Majesty's Commissioners of Inquiry into
        the conditions of the crofters and cottars in the Highlands and
        Islands of Scotland*, Appendix', London, 1884

p.89   'a printed statement . . . although well known in the district'
        Hansard, 29 March, 1886

p.89   'in a constant war . . . and saved the day!' Fr Michael J
        MacDonald, email to the author, February 2010

p.90   'regarded by some . . . I emphatically deny' *Evidence taken
        by Her Majesty's Commissioners of Inquiry into the conditions
        of the crofters and cottars in the Highlands and Islands of
        Scotland*, Appendix, London, 1884

p.90   'a tall, energetic, ascetic . . . Daliburgh, or Dalibrog' *Strange
        Things*, John Lorne Campbell and Trevor H. Hall, 1968

p.91   'the old [chapel] was allowed . . . from within the new' *The
        Catholic Highlands of Scotland*, Odo Blundell, 1917

p.91   'one of the safest . . . to storm-tossed passing vessels' *Ordnance
        Gazetteer of Scotland*, 1882–1885

pp.92–3 'The people of the Outer Isles . . . would have been wealth to
        the poor men and women of the West' *Carmina Gadelica,
        Ortha nan Gaidheal*, Introduction to Volume I, Alexander
        Carmichael, 1900

pp.93–4 'Most of the men would bring their shinty clubs . . . the
        ancient ballads survived better than elsewhere' *The Catholic
        Highlands of Scotland*, Odo Blundell, 1917

p.94   'There is a tradition . . . to render the alms as substantial as
        possible' *Carmina Gadelica, Ortha nan Gaidheal*, Introduction
        to Volume I, Alexander Carmichael, 1900

p.95   'But they have not given up . . . No' *Evidence taken by Her
        Majesty's Commissioners of Inquiry into the conditions of the
        crofters and cottars in the Highlands and Islands of Scotland*,
        Volume I, London, 1884

p.96   'There are two kinds of priests . . . who don't make themselves
        friendly enough' *Father Allan's Island*, Amy Murray, 1918

p.96   'For the first few Sundays . . . something *in* the long fair man!"
        ibid.

p.96   'My boy . . . you'll believe more things' ibid.

p.97   'It has . . . the remedy is in the hands of the ratepayers at
          any ensuing election of the Boards' *Evidence taken by Her
          Majesty's Commissioners of Inquiry into the conditions of the
          crofters and cottars in the Highlands and Islands of Scotland*,
          Appendix, London, 1884

p.97   'the Magna Carta of the Highlands and Islands' John Lorne
          Campbell, preface to *A School in South Uist*, Frederick Rea,
          1964

p.98   'How little I liked to be drawn . . . and degrades his character'
          Allan MacDonald's journal, unpublished

p.99   'took the resolution to cause . . . to frequent such a school any
          longer. . .' *The Catholic Highlands of Scotland*, Odo Blundell,
          1917

pp.100–01 'A few men were grouped . . . kindly but penetrating looks' *A
          School in South Uist*, Frederick Rea, 1964

p.101   'a small, poorly but comfortably . . . every word you say' ibid.

p.102   'at the early age . . . slowly but well' ibid.

p.102   'a barely furnished room . . . then placed in the mouth' ibid.

pp.102–03 'As Father Allan had to say the eleven o'clock Mass . . . which
          sounded very strange to me' ibid.

p.104   'faces showing no other emotion . . . a gun over the head of the
          rest' ibid.

p.105   'Along the road came at full gallop . . . as if it were not worthy
          of comment' ibid.

pp.105–06 'What will we do? . . . head against the wall' *Father Allan's
          Island*, Amy Murray, 1918

pp.106–07 'a mettlesome black horse . . . to indulge in the intellectual
          game of playing chess' *A School in South Uist*, Frederick Rea,
          1964

p.107   'Whatever the distance . . . his own legs' ibid.

p.107   'I saw a tall dark figure . . . a nice trout about a couple of
          pounds' ibid.

p.108   'He often invited different pipers . . . his full six feet height at
          its warlike strains' ibid.

p.108   'Suas e!' *Father Allan's Island*, Amy Murray, 1918

p.108   'a pipe in his mouth, a good fire . . . more or less of most things
          you could mention' ibid.

p.109 'was sparsely furnished . . . to ceiling and end to end of the wall' *A School in South Uist*, Frederick Rea, 1964

p.109 'At present I have nothing . . . painfully alone and poised somewhere in vacuity' Allan MacDonald's journal, unpublished

pp.109–11 'The Congested Districts Board are to give mackerel nets . . . to find out these cases and apply a remedy' *Hansard*, 5 May, 1904

p.112 'unfortunately destroyed to furnish stones . . . the roof was of stone covered over with earth' *Outer Isles*, Ada Goodrich Freer, 1903

p.113 'to be the site of the last battle . . . hence called the Lake of Arms to this day' ibid.

p.114 'Never call a man . . . what isn't likely' *Father Allan's Island*, Amy Murray, 1918

p.114 'once he was settled in . . . away from home after sick calls to remote places' *Father Allan McDonald of Eriskay*, John Lorne Campbell, 1954

pp.115–17 'a gentleman to whom I am indebted . . . I will meditate on the genealogy of St Bridget' *Proceedings of the Gaelic Society of Inverness*, 1892

p.117 'Perhaps no people had a fuller ritual . . . so-called illiterate Highlanders of Scotland' *Carmina Gadelica, Ortha nan Gaidheal*, Introduction to Volume I, Alexander Carmichael, 1900

pp.117–18 'logical critical view . . . politics and prominent men.' - 'A School in South Uist', Frederick Rea, 1964

pp.118–19 'Fr Allan's commentary . . . to teach the eternal truths' Fr Michael J. MacDonald, email to the author, February 2010

p.120 'Though I should stay months here . . . are bound to do the same' *Strange Things*, John Lorne Campbell and Trevor H. Hall, 1968

p.120 'Almost all I know . . . land we have is divided among the people' ibid.

p.121 'Fr Allan is to do the Feinn Saga . . . songs by living poets' ibid.

p.123 'It's time for me to be taking stock' *Eilein na h-Oige, The Poems of Fr Allan McDonald*, Ronald Black (ed.), 2002 p.124   'Below us to the south . . . the gentle soft air' *A School in South Uist*, Frederick Rea, 1964

p.124   'This performance had been . . . the deil made the toon' ibid.

p.125   'At our feet . . . past several smaller islands, was Barra' ibid.

p.125   'Nothing . . . among these poor people.' ibid.

p.126   'Rev. Allan McDonald, besides . . . to collect the necessary funds' - 'The Catholic Highlands of Scotland', Odo Blundell, 1917

pp.126–7 'Father Allan . . . from wrecked or distressed vessels' *A School in South Uist*, Frederick Rea, 1964

pp.127–8 'The life I have gone through . . . as depending on myself and not on God' Allan MacDonald's journal, unpublished

p.128   'S leir dhomh . . . have rescued me from death' *Eilein na h-Oige, The Poems of Fr Allan McDonald* Ronald Black (ed.), 2002

p.128   'I thought it was lack of fervour . . . why didn't you tell me that before?' *Father Allan's Island*, Amy Murray, 1918

CHAPTER SEVEN: ERISKAY

p.131   'Where did all the others . . . From Uist' *Evidence taken by Her Majesty's Commissioners of Inquiry into the conditions of the crofters and cottars in the Highlands and Islands of Scotland*, Volume I, London, 1884

p.131   '[Eriskay] has no road . . . no licensed house upon the island' *The Catholic Highlands of Scotland*, Odo Blundell, 1917

pp.132–3 'Should I even have my choice . . . That keeps unpleasantness outside' *Eilein na h-Oige, The Poems of Fr Allan McDonald*, Ronald Black (ed.), 2002

p.135   'You were so human, angelic . . . would sour your expression' ibid.

p.135   'He had heard . . . after service in church on New Year's Day' *A School in South Uist*, Frederick Rea, 1964

pp.136–7 'At the far end from the open door . . . a blessing they all dispersed' ibid.

p.138   'On the walls, tinted robin's-egg-blue. . . his 'presentation' when he left Dalibrog' *Father Allan's Island*, Amy Murray, 1918 p.139 'When we duly arrived at the priest's house . . . that I had sensed at times among the people' *A School in South Uist*, Frederick Rea, 1964

p.140 'Fire at Ludag . . . I do hope she will recover poor soul' Allan MacDonald's journal, unpublished

p.140 'Poor Roderick MacIntyre, Kilpheder . . . he went to another world quickly' ibid.

p.141 'The South Uist district had still . . . a serious outbreak of typhus fever' *Public Administration in the Highlands and Islands of Scotland*, John Percival Day, 1918

p.142 'The people, panic-stricken . . . the doctor and the priest' ibid.

p.142 'unassisted nursed the sick household . . . to his self-imposed task' *Edinburgh Evening News*, 23rd August 1897

p.143 'I'll take long to forget . . . like a world without sun' *Eilein na h-Oige, The Poems of Fr Allan McDonald*, Ronald Black (ed.), 2002

p.143 'The loss of the want of a thorough friend . . . whoever he be as the brother of Christ' Allan MacDonald's journal, unpublished

p.144 'One year only I look back . . . Society of Priests called the Apostolic Union' ibid.

p.145 'without one absolutely thorough . . . poised somewhere in vacuity' ibid.

p.145 'Preaching was to bring out . . . were to have a special regard for these groups' *Catholic Encyclopaedia*

p.146 'without material to add . . . the ability of walking whither I may get more. . .' Allan MacDonald's journal, unpublished

p.146 'one of the largest . . . that has ever been brought together in Scotland' John Lorne Campbell, introduction to *Gaelic words and expressions from South Uist and Eriskay, collected by Fr. Allan McDonald of Eriskay*, 1958

pp.148–9 'It supplements and completes, on the lexicographical side . . . which make his Collection more readable, perhaps, than any other dictionary' ibid.

p.151 'The Rev Allan Macdonald . . . seem to me to be very beautiful' *Strange Things*, John Lorne Campbell and Trevor H. Hall, 1968 p.154 'Miss Freer is not altogether what she seems . . . to believe in her' - ibid.

p.155 'His life . . . the hermits of old were not more sacrificial, more heroic, than this!' *Outer Isles*, Ada Goodrich Freer, 1903

p.156 'It is the product of far-away thinking . . . of the Highlands and Islands' *Carmina Gadelica, Ortha nan Gaidheal*, Introduction to Volume I, Alexander Carmichael, 1900

p.159 'Till that time . . . 's e rudeigenn a fhuair sinn 'n raoir air son Maighstir Ailean' *The Brave Days*, Neil Munro, 1931

pp.159–61 'enjoying the privileges of British citizenship . . . all that is best and most interesting among the good and interesting people [of the Hebrides]' ibid.

pp.162–3 'Many times . . . are never thrown away, and serve God's purpose anywhere' ibid.

p.163 'He was a man about thirty-five years old . . . and one and equal with the universe?' *Children of Tempest*, Neil Munro, 1903

p.164 'The recital of St Adamnan's "Vision" . . . make it interesting or classical enough to take with them' Allan MacDonald's journal, unpublished

pp.164–5 'Till warmth releases her breath . . . The pure sparkle of the maiden's eye' *Eilein na h-Oige, The Poems of Fr Allan McDonald*, Ronald Black (ed.), 2002

p.166 'held *herself high and her office too . . . and her master carefree, so far as she was able' Father Allan's Island*, Amy Murray, 1918

p.166 'What's that? . . . *What* does he know about us anyway?' - ibid.

pp.166–7 'You'll get dipped yourselves ... He's very witty, you know' ibid.

p.167 'The church is beautiful in design . . . from the Butt of Lewis to the wave-worn cliffs of Barrahead' *The Catholic Highlands of Scotland*, Odo Blundell, 1917

p.168 'I never thought . . . had carried from the beach in their play-hours' *The Brave Days*, Neil Munro, 1931

p.169 'after fervent prayer . . . no small sum in those times' *Father Allan McDonald of Eriskay*, John Lorne Campbell, 1954

p.169 'I waited until . . . and they gave the Church every pennyworth of it' *Father Allan's Island*, Amy Murray, 1918 pp.170–1   'All the able-bodied Catholics in the island ... the cost of the building was £700 over and above the free labour given.' - 'The Catholic Highlands of Scotland', Odo Blundell, 1917

p.173   'The fishermen at his request ... others were provided by the fishermen owners' *Father Allan McDonald of Eriskay*, John Lorne Campbell, 1954

pp.173–4   'It would be hard to find anywhere men ... like to think they can be seeing this' *Father Allan's Island*, Amy Murray, 1918

pp.174–5   'Ascending from the south shore of the little bay ... being enabled to see what is denied to others' *A School in South Uist*, Frederick Rea, 1964

p.176   'He knew ... out of the twentieth century back at least into the 1600s' *A Life of Song*, Marjory Kennedy-Fraser, 1929

pp.176–7   'No fences, no roads ... tolled the bell which called them to worship' ibid.

pp.178–9   'There was no time to be lost ... the little chapel which commanded the harbour' ibid.

pp.181–8   'When Father Allan opened the door to me ... Only send me the songs' *Father Allan's Island*, Amy Murray, 1918

BIBLIOGRAPHY

Bellesheim, Canon Alphons, *History of the Catholic Church of Scotland,* Volume IV, Edinburgh, 1890

Black, Ronald (ed), *Eilein na h-Oige, The Poems of Fr Allan McDonald,* Glasgow, 2002

Blundell, Dom Odo, *The Catholic Highlands of Scotland,* Edinburgh, 1917

Campbell, John Lorne (ed), *Gaelic words and expressions from South Uist and Eriskay, collected by Fr. Allan McDonald of Eriskay,* Oxford, 1958

Campbell, John Lorne and Hall, Trevor H, *Strange Things,* London, 1968

Campbell, John Lorne, *Father Allan McDonald of Eriskay,* Canna, 1954

Carmichael, Alexander, *Carmina Gadelica, Ortha nan Gaidheal,* Volume I, Edinburgh, 1900

Goodrich-Freer, Ada, *Outer Isles,* London, 1903

Kennedy-Fraser, Marjory, *A Life of Song,* Oxford, 1929

Lendrum, Lesley, *Neil Munro, The Biography,* Colonsay, 2004

MacCulloch, Donald B, *Romantic Lochaber, Arisaig and Morar,* Edinburgh, 1939

MacDonald, Father Michael J, 'St Mary's, Bornish: The Story of the Parish and its Priests', unpublished

Macdonald, Father Roddy, *Outline of the History of of the Diocese of Argyll and the Isles,* unpublished

MacGregor, Edith, *The Story of the fort of Fort William,* Fort William, 1954

Maclean, Calum Iain, *The Highlands,* Edinburgh, 1990

Miers, Mary, *The Western Seaboard,* Edinburgh, 2008

Miller, Hugh, *The Cruise of the* Betsey, *with Rambles of a Geologist*, London, 1858

Munro, Neil, *Children of Tempest*, Edinburgh, 1903

Munro, Neil, *The Brave Days*, Edinburgh, 1931

Murray, Amy, *Father Allan's Island*, New York, 1918

Napier, Francis, Lord Napier, et al, *Evidence taken by Her Majesty's Commissioners of Inquiry into the conditions of the crofters and cottars in the Highlands and Islands of Scotland*, Volume I, London, 1884

Rea, Frederick, *A School in South Uist*, London, 1964

Ritchie, Mgr John, *Memorial of Centenary of St Mary's College, Blairs*, London, 1929

Taylor, Maurice, *The Scots College in Spain*, Valladolid, 1971

INDEX

All references in parentheses indicate familial relationship to Father Allan MacDonald.